TIME FOR KIDS
UNITED STATES
ATLAS

CREDITS

TIME FOR KIDS MAGAZINE
MANAGING EDITOR: Martha Pickerill

TIME LEARNING VENTURES
MANAGING EDITOR: Jonathan Rosenbloom
SENIOR EDITOR: Lorin Driggs

BOOK PACKAGER: R Studio T, NYC
ART DIRECTION/DESIGN: Raul Rodriguez and Rebecca Tachna
EDITOR: Curtis Slepian
MAP ARTIST: Tom Camara
COPY EDITOR: Peter McGullam
FACT-CHECKER: Jesse Reiswig

TIME INC. HOME ENTERTAINMENT
PUBLISHER: Richard Fraiman
GENERAL MANAGER: Steven Sandonato
EXECUTIVE DIRECTOR, MARKETING SERVICES: Carol Pittard
DIRECTOR, RETAIL & SPECIAL SALES: Tom Mifsud
DIRECTOR, NEW PRODUCT DEVELOPMENT: Peter Harper
DIRECTOR OF TRADE MARKETING: Sydney Webber
ASSISTANT DIRECTOR, BOOKAZINE MARKETING: Laura Adam
ASSISTANT DIRECTOR, BRAND MARKETING: Joy Butts
ASSOCIATE COUNSEL: Helen Wan
DESIGN & PREPRESS MANAGER: Anne-Michelle Gallero
BOOK PRODUCTION MANAGER: Susan Chodakiewicz
BRAND MANAGER: Shelley Rescober
SPECIAL THANKS TO: Alexandra Bliss, Glenn Buonocore,
Lauren Hall, Jennifer Jacobs, Suzanne Janso, Brynn Joyce,
Robert Marasco, Amy Migliaccio, Brooke Reger,
Ilene Schreider, Adriana Tierno, Alex Voznesenskiy,
Jonathan White
SPECIAL THANKS TO IMAGING:
Patrick Dugan, Neal Clayton, Joseph Agnoli

ISBN 13: 978-1-60320-807-9

ISBN 10: 1-60320-807-0

"TIME For Kids" is a trademark of Time Inc.

We welcome your comments and suggestions
about TIME For Kids Books.

PLEASE WRITE TO US AT:
TIME FOR KIDS BOOKS
ATTENTION: BOOK EDITORS
PO BOX 11016
DES MOINES, IA 50336-1016

If you would like to order
any of our hardcover
Collector's Edition books,
please call us at 1-800-327-6388.
(Monday through Friday,
7:00 a.m.– 8:00 p.m. or
Saturday, 7:00 a.m.– 6:00 p.m.
Central Time).

Contents

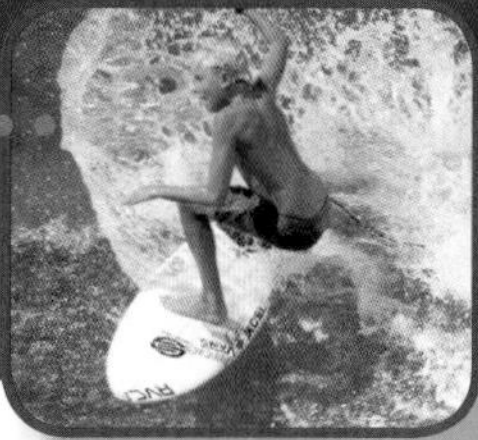

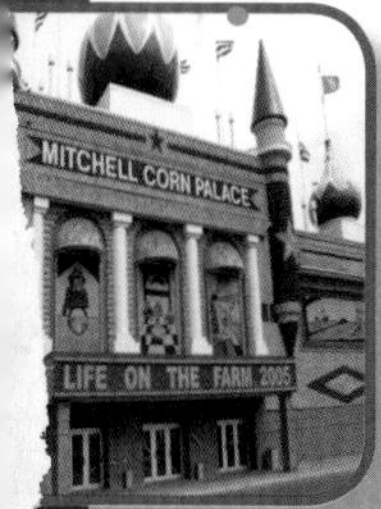

MITCHELL CORN PALACE

LIFE ON THE FARM 2005

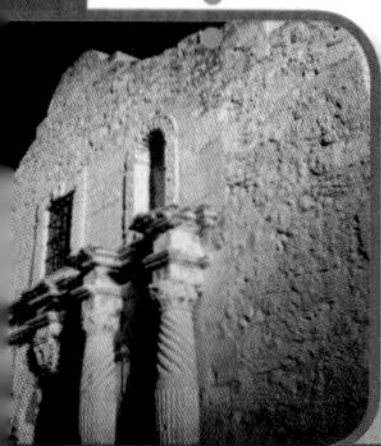

How to Use the TFK U.S. Atlas

Take a road trip across the country with the **TIME FOR KIDS U.S. ATLAS**. The book divides the nation into regions and states. Each section begins with a map of a U.S. region and a description of its features. It's followed by maps of every state within that region. "Fact File" and "Did You Know?" give information about regions and states, including statistics, history and landmarks. "Roadside Fun" offers a look at of some unusual places that may be worth a detour. At the back of the book, "U.S. Facts" gives vital statistics on the nation as a whole. The Glossary defines some of the terms used in the atlas. There are also puzzles that test the "state" of your knowledge. But before you begin your journey through the states, take a step back and view the entire U.S. on maps located on pages 6 through 15.

ABBREVIATIONS

cm	centimeter
ha	hectare
kg	kilogram
L	liter
Mt.	Mount
Mts.	Mountains
m	meter
mi	mile
R.	River
sq km	square kilometer
sq mi	square mile
St.	Saint

KEY TO MAP SYMBOLS

- ✪ state capital
- ✪ U.S. capital
- ● city
- ▲ mountain or volcano

Introduction
These paragraphs give a brief overview of the region.

Fact File
Look here for important information about a region's states and cities. Population numbers are taken from U.S. Census estimates.

Did You Know?
These are cool facts about the region and its states.

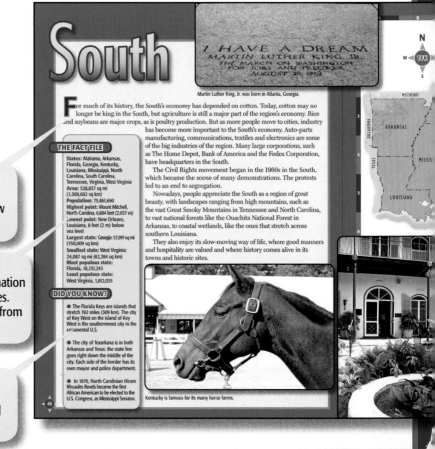

South

Martin Luther King, Jr. was born in Atlanta, Georgia.

For much of its history, the South's economy has depended on cotton. Today, cotton may no longer be king in the South, but agriculture is still a major part of the region's economy. Rice and soybeans are major crops, as is poultry production. But as more people move to cities, industry has become more important to the South's economy. Auto-parts manufacturing, communications, textiles and electronics are some of the big industries of the region. Many large corporations, such as The Home Depot, Bank of America and the Fedex Corporation, have headquarters in the South.

The Civil Rights movement began in the 1960s in the South, which became the scene of many demonstrations. The protests led to an end to segregation.

Nowadays, people appreciate the South as a region of great beauty, with landscapes ranging from high mountains, such as the vast Great Smoky Mountains in Tennessee and North Carolina, to vast national forests like the Ouachita National Forest in Arkansas, to coastal wetlands, like the ones that stretch across southern Louisiana.

They also enjoy its slow-moving way of life, where good manners and hospitality are valued and where history comes alive in its towns and historic sites.

THE FACT FILE

States: Alabama, Arkansas, Florida, Georgia, Kentucky, Louisiana, Mississippi, North Carolina, South Carolina, Tennessee, Virginia, West Virginia
Area: 528,837 sq mi (1,369,682 sq km)
Population: 75,861,690
Highest point: Mount Mitchell, North Carolina, 6,684 feet (2,037 m)
Lowest point: New Orleans, Louisiana, 8 feet (2 m) below sea level
Largest state: Georgia: 57,919 sq mi (150,009 sq km)
Smallest state: West Virginia: 24,087 sq mi (62,384 sq km)
Most populous state: Florida, 18,251,243
Least populous state: West Virginia, 1,812,035

DID YOU KNOW?

● The Florida Keys are islands that stretch 192 miles (309 km). The city of Key West on the island of Key West is the southernmost city in the continental U.S.

● The city of Texarkana is in both Arkansas and Texas: the state line goes right down the middle of the city. Each side of the border has its own mayor and police department.

● In 1870, North Carolinian Hiram Rhoades Revels became the first African American to be elected to the U.S. Congress, as Mississippi Senator.

Kentucky is famous for its many horse farms.

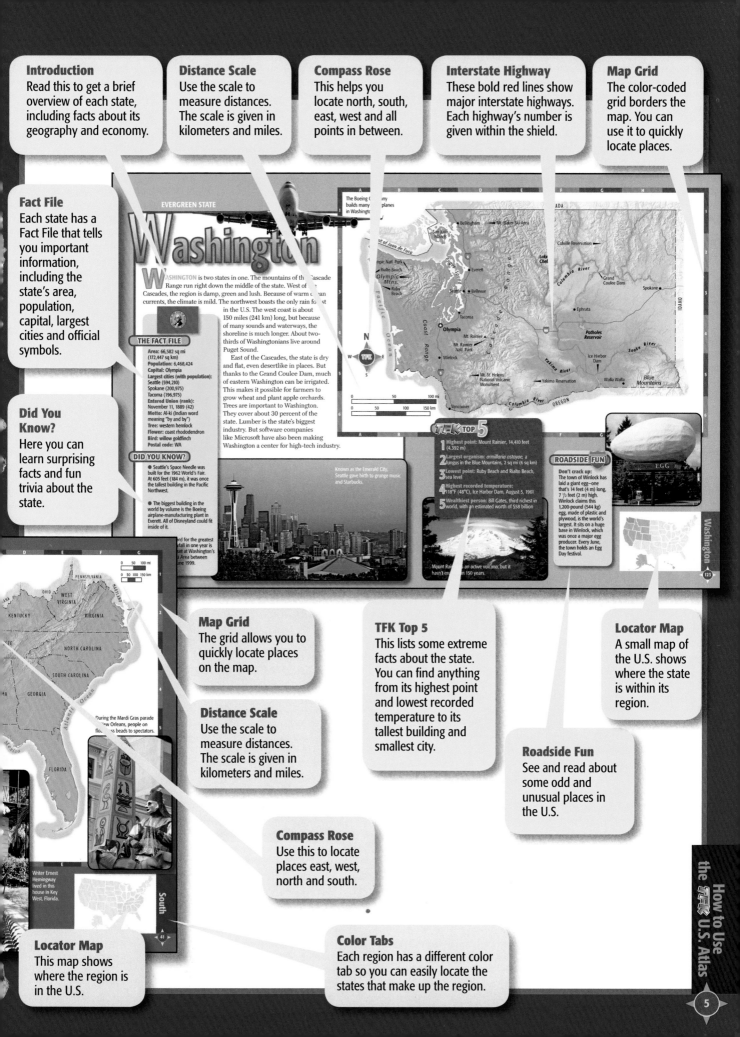

Introduction
Read this to get a brief overview of each state, including facts about its geography and economy.

Distance Scale
Use the scale to measure distances. The scale is given in kilometers and miles.

Compass Rose
This helps you locate north, south, east, west and all points in between.

Interstate Highway
These bold red lines show major interstate highways. Each highway's number is given within the shield.

Map Grid
The color-coded grid borders the map. You can use it to quickly locate places.

Fact File
Each state has a Fact File that tells you important information, including the state's area, population, capital, largest cities and official symbols.

Did You Know?
Here you can learn surprising facts and fun trivia about the state.

Map Grid
The grid allows you to quickly locate places on the map.

Distance Scale
Use the scale to measure distances. The scale is given in kilometers and miles.

TFK Top 5
This lists some extreme facts about the state. You can find anything from its highest point and lowest recorded temperature to its tallest building and smallest city.

Locator Map
A small map of the U.S. shows where the state is within its region.

Roadside Fun
See and read about some odd and unusual places in the U.S.

Compass Rose
Use this to locate places east, west, north and south.

Locator Map
This map shows where the region is in the U.S.

Color Tabs
Each region has a different color tab so you can easily locate the states that make up the region.

EVERGREEN STATE

Washington

WASHINGTON is two states in one. The mountains of the Cascade Range run right down the middle of the state. West of the Cascades, the region is damp, green and lush. Because of warm ocean currents, the climate is mild. The northwest boasts the only rain forest in the U.S. The west coast is about 150 miles (241 km) long, but because of many sounds and waterways, the shoreline is much longer. About two-thirds of Washingtonians live around Puget Sound.

East of the Cascades, the state is dry and flat, even desertlike in places. But thanks to the Grand Coulee Dam, much of eastern Washington can be irrigated. This makes it possible for farmers to grow wheat and plant apple orchards. Trees are important to Washington. They cover about 30 percent of the state. Lumber is the state's biggest industry. But software companies like Microsoft have also been making Washington a center for high-tech industry.

THE FACT FILE
Area: 66,582 sq mi (172,447 sq km)
Population: 6,468,424
Capital: Olympia
Largest cities (with population):
Seattle (594,210)
Spokane (200,975)
Tacoma (196,975)
Entered Union (rank):
November 11, 1889 (42)
Motto: Al-ki (Indian word meaning "by and by")
Tree: western hemlock
Flower: coast rhododendron
Bird: willow goldfinch
Postal code: WA

DID YOU KNOW?
● Seattle's Space Needle was built for the 1962 World's Fair. At 605 feet (184 m), it was once the tallest building in the Pacific Northwest.

● The biggest building in the world by volume is the Boeing airplane-manufacturing plant in Everett. All of Disneyland could fit inside of it.

The Boeing Company builds many of its planes in Washington.

Known as the Emerald City, Seattle gave birth to grunge music and Starbucks.

TFK TOP 5
1 Highest point: Mount Rainier, 14,410 feet (4,392 m)
2 Largest organism: armillaria ostoyae, a fungus in the Blue Mountains, 2 sq mi (6 sq km)
3 Lowest point: Ruby Beach and Rialto Beach, sea level
4 Highest recorded temperature: 118°F (48°C), Ice Harbor Dam, August 5, 1961
5 Wealthiest person: Bill Gates, third richest in world, with an estimated worth of $58 billion

Mount Rainier is an active volcano, but it hasn't erupted in 150 years.

ROADSIDE FUN
Don't crack up: The town of Winlock has laid a giant egg—one that's 14 feet (4 m) long, 7½ feet (2 m) high. Winlock claims this 1,200-pound (544 kg) egg, made of plastic and plywood, is the world's largest. It sits on a huge base in Winlock, which was once a major egg producer. Every June, the town holds an Egg Day festival.

EGG

During the Mardi Gras parade in New Orleans, people on floats toss beads to spectators.

Writer Ernest Hemingway lived in this house in Key West, Florida.

South
41

The U.S.

A political map shows the borders that separate states and regions. It is called "political" because governments create boundaries between areas.

A political map, like the one on this page, shows key cities and state capitals. The United States is made up of 50 states, 49 of which are part of the North American continent. One state, Hawaii, is in the Pacific Ocean. Alaska is separated by Canada from the 48 contiguous states. These 48 states are known as the continental U.S. and also as the Lower 48.

Because there isn't enough room to fit Alaska and Hawaii in this map of the U.S., the two states are shown at the bottom of the page. State capitals are indicated by a star. Washington, D.C. (D.C. stands for "District of Columbia"), the capital of the U.S., is indicated by a larger star. Located between Maryland and Virginia, it is a city, not a state, but not part of any other state.

DID YOU KNOW?

● The United States is divided into six time zones: From east to west, they are eastern, central, mountain, Pacific, Alaskan and Hawaiian-Aleutian (including Hawaii and most of the Aleutian Islands). U.S. territories are in three other time zones: Atlantic (Puerto Rico and the U.S. Virgin Islands), Samoa (American Samoa) and Chamorro (Guam and the Northern Mariana Islands).

CANADA

Seattle
WASHINGTON
Olympia
Columbia River
MONTANA
Helena
Billings
Portland
Salem
OREGON
IDAHO
Boise
Cascade Range
Rocky
WYOMING
Casper
Cheyenne
Great Salt Lake
Salt Lake City
West Valley City
UTAH
NEVADA
Carson City
Mountains
COLOR
Sacramento
Sierra Nevada
Colorado River
Pacific Ocean
San Francisco
San Jose
CALIFORNIA
Las Vegas
Santa Fe
Albuquerque
NEW MEX
ARIZONA
Los Angeles
Phoenix
San Diego
Tucson
MEXICO

0   200 mi
0   300 km

Note: Alaska and Hawaii are not shown in their true locations and not drawn to scale.

ALASKA
Bering Sea
CANADA
Anchorage
Juneau
Gulf of Alaska
Aleutian Islands

When it's 6 a.m. at Waikiki Beach in Honolulu, Hawaii,...

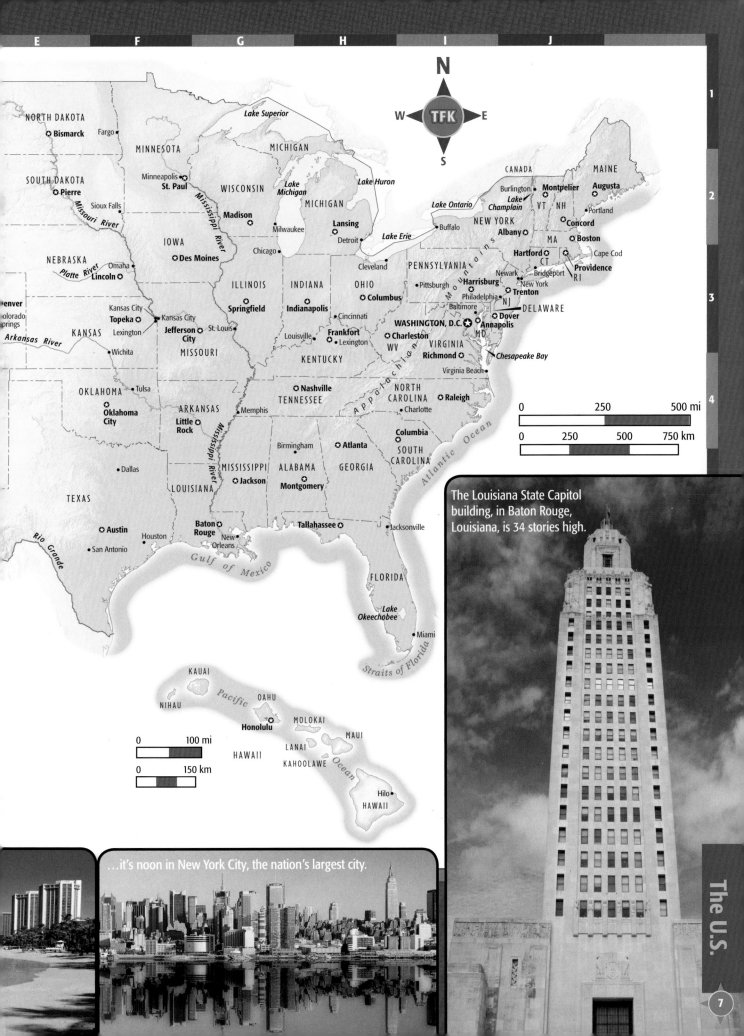

The Louisiana State Capitol building, in Baton Rouge, Louisiana, is 34 stories high.

...it's noon in New York City, the nation's largest city.

The U.S.

The Lower 48 states of the United States are bordered by the Atlantic Ocean to the east, the Straits of Florida to the southeast, Mexico and the Gulf of Mexico to the south, the Pacific Ocean to the west, and Canada to the north. Canada also forms the southern and eastern boundaries of Alaska, and the Bering Sea and the Arctic Ocean form its west and north borders, respectively. The U.S. is the second largest North American nation in area, after Canada. And it is the world's third largest nation in both land area and population.

The U.S. has a great variety of geographical features, from huge lakes to deserts, from thick forests and coastal swamps to grass-covered plains and rugged mountain ranges. A physical map, like the one here, shows those geographical features. It is also a relief map, meaning it indicates the elevation, or height, of the land. In this map, the blue areas are water, the green areas have the lowest elevation, and the tan and brown areas have a higher elevation.

D YOU KNOW?

- The Continental Divide of the U.S. is a ridge of high ground that runs north and south through the Rocky Mountains. On the west side of the divide, streams run to the west, and on the east side they flow east. Waters that flow east empty into the Atlantic Ocean, mostly by way of the Gulf of Mexico. The waters flowing west empty into the Pacific Ocean.

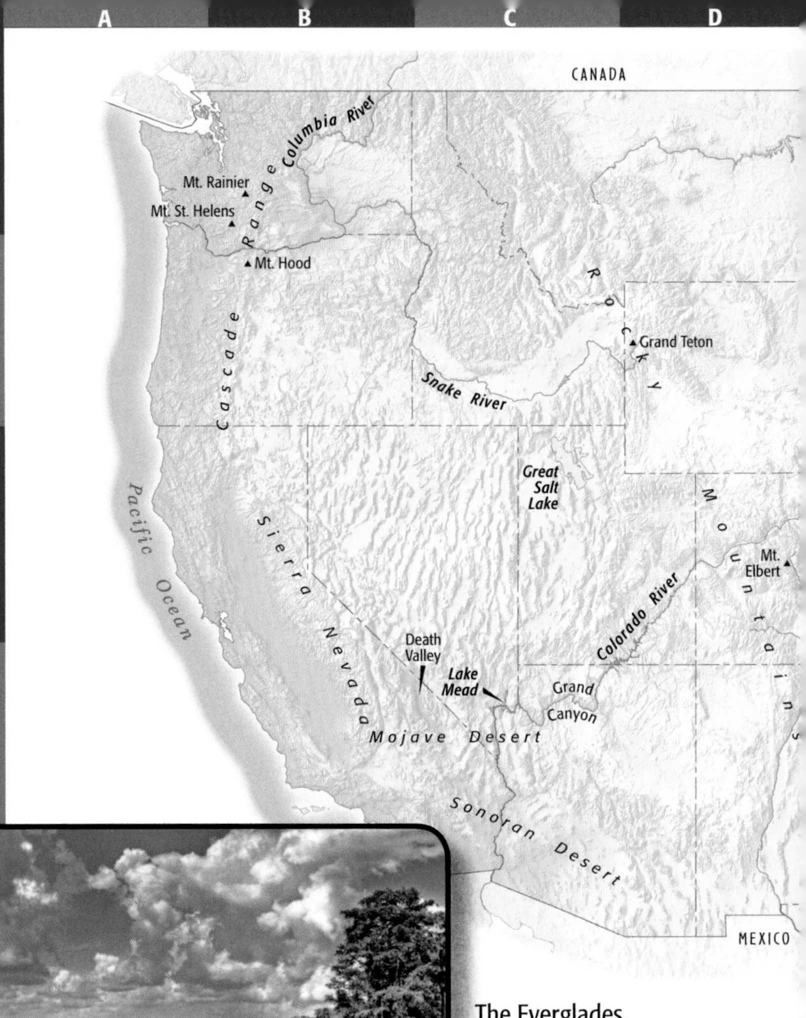
A
B
C
D
1
2
3
4
7
8
CANADA
Columbia River
Mt. Rainier
Mt. St. Helens
Mt. Hood
Cascade Range
Rocky Mountains
Grand Teton
Snake River
Great Salt Lake
Pacific Ocean
Sierra Nevada
Mt. Elbert
Colorado River
Death Valley
Lake Mead
Grand Canyon
Mojave Desert
Sonoran Desert
MEXICO
Brooks Range
Bering Sea
Mt. McKinley (Denali)
Alaska Range
CANADA
0 200 mi
0 300 km
Alaska Peninsula
Gulf of Alaska
Alexander Archipelago
Aleutian Islands

The Everglades, in Florida, covers about 4,000 sq mi (10,000 sq km).

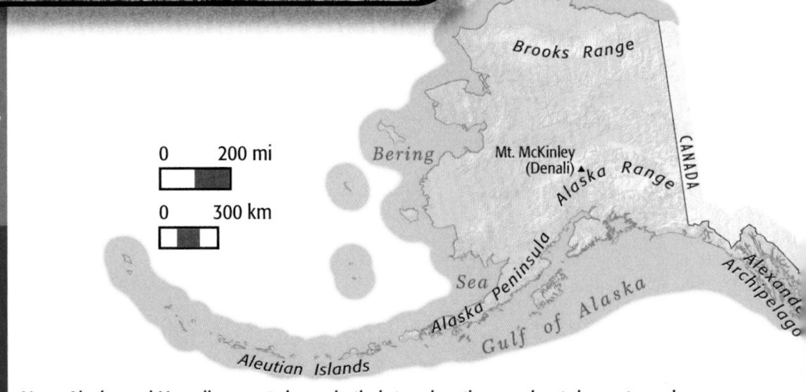

Note: Alaska and Hawaii are not shown in their true locations and not drawn to scale.

The Grand Canyon is 6,000 feet (1,828 m) at its deepest point and 15 miles (24 km) at its widest.

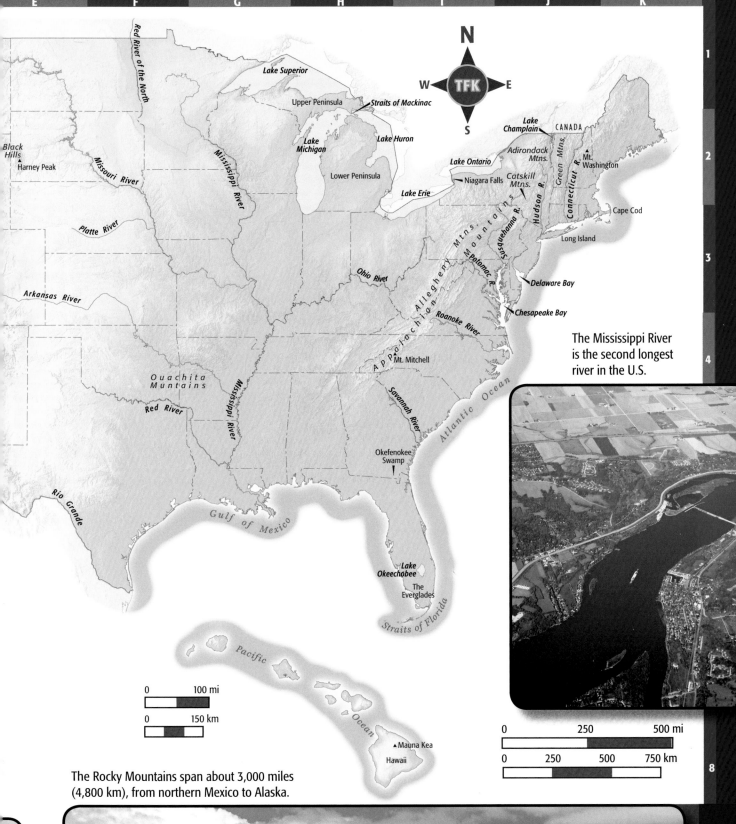

Red River of the North

Black
Hills
▲ Harney Peak

Missouri River

Platte River

Arkansas River

Rio Grande

Red River

Ouachita
Muntains

Mississippi River

Lake Superior

Upper Peninsula

Lake
Michigan

Lower Peninsula

Lake Huron

Straits of Mackinac

Lake Ontario

Lake Erie

Niagara Falls

Ohio River

Appalachian Mountains

Allegheny Mtns.

Mt. Mitchell ▲

Roanoke River

Savannah River

Okefenokee
Swamp

Lake
Okeechobee

The
Everglades

Straits of Florida

Gulf of Mexico

Mississippi River

N
W   TFK   E
S

Lake
Champlain

CANADA

Adirondack
Mtns.

Catskill
Mtns.

Green Mtns.

Mt.
Washington ▲

Susquehanna R.

Hudson R.

Connecticut R.

Cape Cod

Long Island

Potomac R.

Delaware Bay

Chesapeake Bay

Atlantic Ocean

The Mississippi River
is the second longest
river in the U.S.

Pacific

Ocean

▲ Mauna Kea

Hawaii

0   100 mi
0   150 km

0   250   500 mi
0   250   500   750 km

1

2

3

4

8

The Rocky Mountains span about 3,000 miles
(4,800 km), from northern Mexico to Alaska.

The U.S.

The United States of America started out fairly small but ended up very large. At the end of the Revolutionary War, the U.S. was made up of 13 states, as well as land that reached as far west as the Mississippi River. This included the Northwest Territory, which was later broken up into smaller territories that eventually became Ohio, Indiana and other Midwestern states.

The U.S didn't stop its growth at the Mississippi River. The nation kept adding land through purchases, treaties, Acts of Congress and military force. Here are some highlights of the country's expansion: In 1803, the U.S. purchased the Louisiana Territory from France for $15 million. The land, which extended to the Rocky Mountains, nearly doubled the size of the U.S. In 1819, Spain gave Florida to the U.S. in exchange for the U.S.'s promise to pay claims against Spain for up to $5 million. In 1845, the U.S. annexed, or took over, the Republic of Texas. Some of that land was sold to the U.S. by Texas in 1850. In 1846, a treaty with Great Britain gave the U.S. a huge section of the west called the Oregon Country. The land later became Idaho, Oregon and Washington, as well as parts of other states. At the end of the Mexican War in 1848, Mexico sold to the U.S. what is today California, Nevada, Utah, most of New Mexico and Arizona, and parts of Colorado and Wyoming. Five years later in 1853, land gained from Mexico in the Gadsden Purchase filled out the continental U.S.

DID YOU KNOW?

The Northwest Ordinance was an early act of the U.S. before the passing of the Constitution. It explained how a territory could become a state. These were the steps:

● The U.S. government appoints officials to rule over a territory.

● When the population of voters reaches 5,000, the territory holds an election to create a legislature.

● When the population reaches 60,000, the territory writes a state constitution and applies to the U.S. Congress to become a state.

● If Congress approves, the President proclaims the territory a state.

Note: Alaska and Hawaii are not shown in their true locations and not drawn to scale.

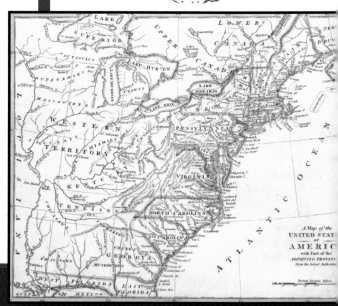

This early map of the United States was printed in England in 1795.

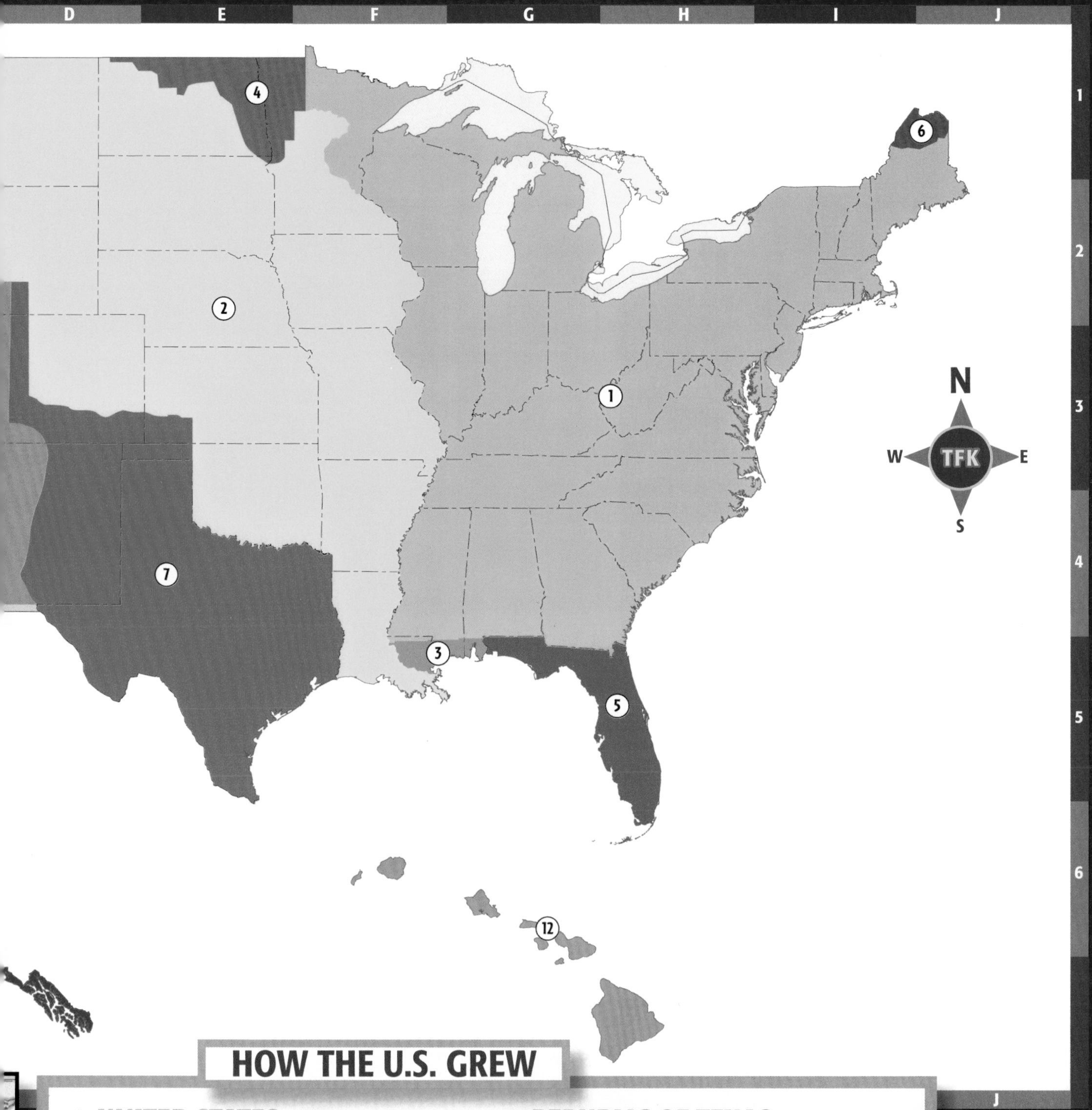

N
W ← TFK → E
S

HOW THE U.S. GREW

1. UNITED STATES, 1783

2. LOUISIANA PURCHASE, BOUGHT FROM FRANCE, 1803

3. WEST FLORIDA, ANNEXED FROM SPAIN, 1810–1813

4. RED RIVER BASIN, CLAIMED BY GREAT BRITAIN UNTIL 1842

5. FLORIDA, PURCHASED FROM SPAIN, 1819

6. CLAIMED BY BRITAIN UNTIL 1842

7. REPUBLIC OF TEXAS, ANNEXED, 1845

8. OREGON COUNTRY, JOINTLY CLAIMED BY GREAT BRITAIN AND U.S. UNTIL 1846

9. GIVEN UP BY MEXICO, 1848

10. GADSDEN PURCHASE, FROM MEXICO, 1853

11. ALASKA PURCHASE, FROM RUSSIA, 1867

12. HAWAIIAN ANNEXATION, 1898

The U.S.

675010 ADMIT ONE 675010

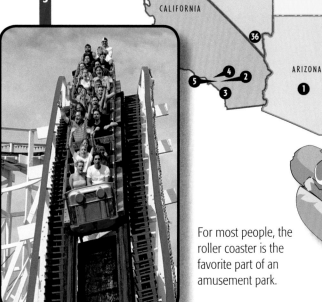

People have been having fun at U.S. amusement parks for a long time. The oldest continuously operating amusement park in the U.S., called Lake Compounce, was built in 1846 in Bristol, Connecticut. Some say the first true theme park was Santa Claus Town, which opened in 1935 in Santa Claus, Indiana, and had attractions based on one theme (Santa, of course). In 1946, the park became Santa Claus Land (and is today called Holiday World). Another candidate for first true amusement park is Knott's Berry Farm, which opened in 1940 in Buena Vista, California, and is still going strong.

Today, there are more than 400 amusement parks spread all over the country that are visited by about 335 million people each year. The Magic Kingdom at Walt Disney World in Orlando, Florida, is the most popular (and largest) amusement park in the world. But amusement parks come in all sizes and types. The map on this page shows the location of some of the most popular amusement parks in the U.S.

DID YOU KNOW?

● There are more than 1,300 roller coasters in the U.S. The tallest and fastest coaster is Kingda Ka at Six Flags Great Adventure in Jackson, New Jersey. It is 456 feet (138 m) tall and reaches a speed of 128 mph (206 km/h).

● According to the International Association of Amusement Parks, the favorite amusement park foods are, in order of preference: funnel cake, ice cream, pizza, hot dogs and cotton candy.

Funnel cake is one of the favorite taste treats for visitors to amusement parks.

For most people, the roller coaster is the favorite part of an amusement park.

1. Castles N' Coasters, Phoenix, Arizona
2. Disneyland, Anaheim, California
3. Legoland, Carlsbad, California
4. Universal Studios, Hollywood, California
5. Knott's Berry Farm, Buena Vista, California
6. Water World, Denver, Colorado
7. Lakeside Amusement Park, Denver, Colorado
8. Quassy Amusement Park, Middlebury, Connecticut
9. Walt Disney World, Orlando, Florida
10. Discovery Cove, Orlando, Florida
11. Islands of Adventure, Orlando, Florida
12. Universal Studios, Orlando, Florida
13. Six Flags Over Georgia, Austell, Georgia
14. Six Flags White Water, Atlanta, Georgia
15. Wild Adventures, Valdosta, Georgia
16. Silverwood Theme Park and Boulder Beach Water Park, Coeur d'Alene, Idaho
17. Holiday World & Splashin' Safari, Santa Claus, Indiana
18. Iowa State Fair, Des Moines, Iowa [has rides]
19. Beech Bend Park, Bowling Green, Kentucky
20. Crossroads Village & Huckleberry Railroad, Flint, Michigan

Thrill rides come in all shapes and sizes.

21. Trimper's Amusement Park, Ocean City, Maryland
22. Funtown Splashtown, Saco, Maine
23. Worlds of Fun, Kansas City, Missouri
24. Water Park of America, Bloomington, Minnesota
25. Knott's Camp Snoopy at the Mall of America, Minneapolis, Minnesota
26. Valleyfair, Shakopee, Minnesota
27. Big Sky Waterpark, Columbia Falls, Montana
28. Paramount's Carowinds, Charlotte, North Carolina
29. Astroland Amusement Park, Brooklyn, New York
30. Playland, Rye, New York
31. Six Flags Great Adventure & Wild Safari, Jackson, New Jersey
32. Water Country, Portsmouth, New Hampshire
33. Canobie Lake Park, Salem, New Hampshire
34. Cliff's Amusement Park, Albuquerque, New Mexico
35. Carousel Gardens Amusement Park, New Orleans, Louisiana
36. Terrible's Primm Valley Casino Resorts, Primm, Nevada
37. Paramount Kings Islands, Kings Island, Ohio
38. Cedar Point, Sandusky, Ohio
39. Frontier City, Oklahoma City, Oklahoma
40. Oaks Amusement Park, Portland, Oregon

41. Idlewild Park, Ligonier, Pennsylvania
42. Hersheypark, Hershey, Pennsylvania
43. Dorney Park & Wildwater Kingdom, Allentown, Pennsylvania
44. Knoebels, Elysburg, Pennsylvania
45. Kennywood Park, Pittsburgh, Pennsylvania
46. Lakemont Park & Island Waterpark, Altoona, Pennsylvania
47. Myrtle Beach Pavilion Amusement Park, Myrtle Beach, South Carolina
48. SeaWorld, San Antonio, Texas
49. Six Flags Over Texas, Arlington, Texas
50. Dollywood, Pigeon Forge, Tennessee
51. Lagoon Amusement Park, Farmington, Utah
52. Liberty Land Fun Center, Lehi, Utah
53. Busch Gardens, Williamsburg, Virginia
54. Kings Dominion, Doswell, Virginia
55. Great Vermont Corn Maze, Danville, Vermont
56. Mt. Olympus Water & Theme Park, Wisconsin Dells, Wisconsin
57. Bay Beach Amusement Park, Green Bay, Wisconsin
58. Camden Park, Huntington, West Virginia

The U.S. at Night

This map shows the continental U.S. from space at night. The little white dots are the lights made by large towns and cities across the U.S. NASA used information from orbiting satellites to create the photo. The satellites were meant to record moonlight reflecting off clouds. That data helps planes navigate at night. But when there was a new moon (a period when the moon is dark), the clouds didn't light up. Instead, scientists discovered that the satellites could detect lights on the ground.

The brightest areas on the map are the ones with the most cities. The thin lines connecting the brighter dots are interstate highways. NASA scientists use maps like this to see how urban areas are spreading across the land. They compare night maps to maps that show Earth's soil and plant life. This lets them understand the effects that growing urban areas have on our natural resources.

DID YOU KNOW?

● The percentage of people who live in cities in the U.S. has gone from 39 percent at the beginning of the 20th century to 80 percent today. Cities are taking up more and more land. For example, between 1980 and 1997, the U.S. lost more than 26 million sq mi (67 million sq km) of rural land to towns, cities and suburbs. That's an area larger than the entire state of West Virginia.

Northeast

The **NORTHEAST** is the birthplace of the United States. The region is the site of many of the first English settlements and is where the idea of nationhood took hold. Among its states are nine of the 13 original colonies, and on its land much of the Revolutionary War was fought. A region within the Northeast is New England, which comprises six states: Maine, New Hampshire, Vermont, Massachusetts, Rhode Island and Connecticut. These states have similar "Yankee" histories, culture and geography.

South and west of New England are the Mid-Atlantic states of New York, New Jersey, Pennsylvania, Delaware and Maryland. Some of the largest U.S cities, such as New York City, Baltimore and Philadelphia, are found in this region.

Not all of the Northeast is urban. Much of the area is rich in farmlands, particularly upstate New York, New Jersey, Connecticut and Pennsylvania. The region has snow-covered mountains and large forests, huge bays, high waterfalls, powerful rivers and beautiful beaches. The landscape of the Northeast is varied and scenic.

THE FACT FILE

States: Connecticut, Delaware, Maine, Maryland, Massachusetts, New Hampshire, New Jersey, New York, Pennsylvania, Rhode Island, Vermont
Area: 181,508 sq mi (470,103 sq km)
Population: 61,163,734
Highest point: Mount Washington, New Hampshire, 6,288 feet (1,917 m)
Lowest point: sea level at the Atlantic Coast
Largest state: New York, 53,097 sq mi (137,521 sq km)
Smallest state: Rhode Island, 1,045 sq mi (2,706 sq km)
Most populous state: New York, 19,297,729
Least populous state: Vermont, 621,254
Most populous city: New York City, 8,274,527

DID YOU KNOW?

● Lake Placid, New York, was the site of the 1980 Winter Olympics, where the underdog U.S. men's hockey team won the gold medal.

● The fastest wind ever recorded was 231 mph (371 km/h) on Mount Washington, New Hampshire, in 1934.

● Syracuse, New York, is the Northeast's snowiest city—its average annual snowfall is 110 inches (279 cm).

Bruce Springsteen often sings songs about his native New Jersey.

There are 3,600 species of plants, fish, birds and mammals in and around the Chesapeake Bay.

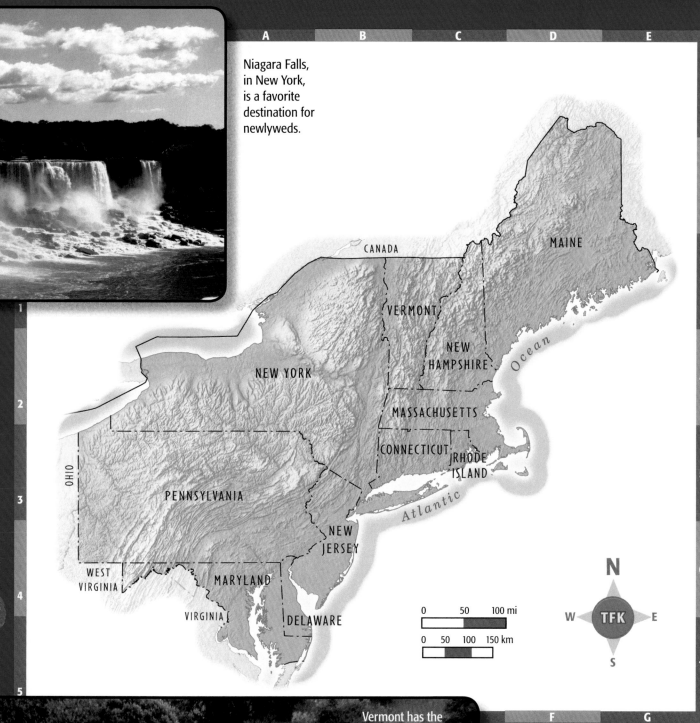

Niagara Falls, in New York, is a favorite destination for newlyweds.

CANADA

MAINE

VERMONT

NEW HAMPSHIRE

Ocean

NEW YORK

MASSACHUSETTS

OHIO

CONNECTICUT

RHODE ISLAND

PENNSYLVANIA

Atlantic

NEW JERSEY

WEST VIRGINIA

MARYLAND

VIRGINIA

DELAWARE

0   50   100 mi

0   50   100   150 km

N
W — TFK — E
S

F   G

Vermont has the highest ratio of cows to people in the U.S.—about one cow to four people.

Northeast

Connecticut

CONNECTICUT may be the third smallest state in area, but its population is tops in average income. The southwestern part of the state is called the Gold Coast because it is the location of many prosperous towns, such as Greenwich, Westport and Darien. Many of their residents commute to nearby New York City. Beautiful estates dot lush land in the northwest. The middle of the state, the area around Hartford, is another large population center. Many people there make their living manufacturing everything from jet engines and electronics to sewing machines. Others work for the numerous insurance companies headquartered in the state.

It may have some large cities, but Connecticut has a rural feel. The state is full of rolling hills, pastures and small, quaint towns. People sail the 90-mile (145 km) length of Long Island Sound or enjoy the more than 60 state parks and forests. The rugged northwest region has many forested hills and ridges. The stony northeast, or Eastern Highlands, is also full of wooded hills. Much of the state's terrain is rocky, making it hard to grow crops, but dairy farms thrive. It's the beauty of the land, not its products, that makes Connecticut so appealing.

THE FACT FILE

Area: 4,846 sq mi (12,550 sq km)
Population: 3,502,309
Capital: Hartford
Largest cities (with population):
Bridgeport (136,695)
Hartford (124,563)
New Haven (123,932)
Entered Union (rank):
January 9, 1788 (5)
Motto: *Qui transtulit sustinet* (He who transplanted still sustains)
Tree: white oak
Flower: mountain laurel
Bird: American robin
Postal code: CT

DID YOU KNOW?

● In 1878, the world's first telephone directory was published in New Haven. It had only 50 names.

● In 1901, Connecticut passed the first speed-limit law for cars in the U.S. It set a speed limit of 12 mph (19 km/h) in cities.

● Mark Twain, one of America's greatest writers, lived in a beautiful brick house in Hartford from 1874 to 1891. It was here that he wrote *Adventures of Huckleberry Finn.* The Twain House & Museum is open to the public.

Founded in 1701, Yale University, in New Haven, is one of the most renowned universities in the world.

NEW YORK

4

5

6

Stamford
Greenwich

A   B

Visitors can tour Mark Twain's Hartford home.

Bear Mountain

MASSACHUSETTS

Litchfield Hills

N
W TFK E
S

91

84

Willimantic River

Hartford ★

Coventry •

RHODE ISLAND

New Britain •

Connecticut River

Candlewood Lake

Waterbury •

84

91

Housatonic River

Norwich •

Danbury

New Haven •

Lake Gaillard

New London • • Groton

95

Orange •

Long Island Sound

Bridgeport •

95

Vestport •

lk •

0		25		50 mi

0	25	50	75 km

TFK TOP 5

1 Highest point: south slope of Mount Frissell, 2,380 feet (725 m)

2 Lowest point: sea level, at Long Island Sound

3 Lowest recorded temperature: -32°F (-35°C), Coventry, January 22, 1961

4 Tallest building: City Place, Hartford, 535 feet (163 m)

5 Largest human-made lake: Candlewood Lake, 9 sq mi (23 sq km)

There are many beautiful houses on the Connecticut shore of Long Island Sound.

Connecticut

Delaware

Except for its northern tip, **DELAWARE** is part of a flat, low-lying region called the Atlantic Coastal Plain. The state's average elevation—60 feet (18 m)—is the lowest in the U.S. Because the land is so close to sea level, swamps and marshes abound, the biggest being Cypress Swamp (also known as the Great Pocomoke Swamp). Delaware may be small—the second smallest state in the Union—and flat, but it stands tall in our nation's history as the first state to ratify the U.S. Constitution, in 1787.

Most of Delaware's cities are located in the north, above the Chesapeake and Delaware Canal. About two-thirds of the state's population lives in and around Wilmington, headquarters of the giant chemical company DuPont. DuPont is a major employer, as are credit-card companies and banks.

Rural southern Delaware, which makes up about two-thirds of the state, is mostly farmland. Soybeans, corn and potatoes are important crops, but the main farm products are chickens and eggs. The Atlantic coastline is only 28 miles (45 km) long, and people enjoy every inch of it. Rehoboth Beach is one of the most popular vacation spots in the region, especially for people from Washington, D.C. Cape Henlopen State Park has large sand dunes and beautiful nature trails.

THE FACT FILE

Area: 1,955 sq mi (5,153 sq km)
Population: 864,764
Capital: Dover
Largest cities (with population):
Wilmington (72,868)
Dover (35,811)
Newark (29,992)
Entered Union (rank):
December 7, 1787 (1)
Motto: Liberty and independence
Tree: American holly
Flower: peach blossom
Bird: blue hen chicken
Postal code: DE

DID YOU KNOW?

● Delaware is the only state without any land, memorials or sites belonging to the National Park System.

● The first paved highway in Delaware is the DuPont Highway. It was finished in 1934 and stretches about 96 miles (154 km) across the length of the state. The highway was named after the president of the DuPont chemical company, Coleman duPont, who paid for the highway with his own money.

● Delaware has three counties— New Castle, Kent and Sussex—the fewest of any state. (Alaska is divided into boroughs and Louisiana is divided into parishes.)

The sands of Rehoboth Beach

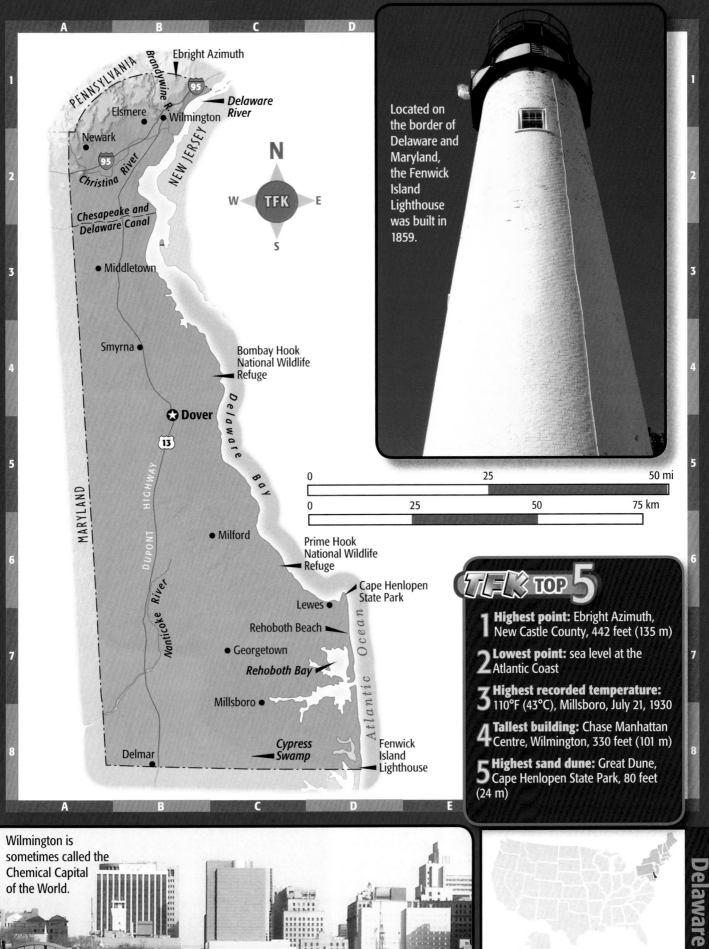

Ebright Azimuth

PENNSYLVANIA

Brandywine R.

Elsmere ·

· Wilmington

Delaware River

Newark ·

NEW JERSEY

Christina River

N

W TFK **E**

S

Chesapeake and Delaware Canal

· Middletown

MARYLAND

Smyrna ·

Bombay Hook National Wildlife Refuge

DUPONT HIGHWAY

★ **Dover**

Delaware Bay

· Milford

Prime Hook National Wildlife Refuge

Nanticoke River

Cape Henlopen State Park

Lewes ·

Rehoboth Beach

· Georgetown

Rehoboth Bay

Atlantic Ocean

Millsboro ·

Cypress Swamp

Delmar ·

Fenwick Island Lighthouse

0   25   50 mi

0   25   50   75 km

Located on the border of Delaware and Maryland, the Fenwick Island Lighthouse was built in 1859.

TFK TOP 5

1 **Highest point:** Ebright Azimuth, New Castle County, 442 feet (135 m)

2 **Lowest point:** sea level at the Atlantic Coast

3 **Highest recorded temperature:** 110°F (43°C), Millsboro, July 21, 1930

4 **Tallest building:** Chase Manhattan Centre, Wilmington, 330 feet (101 m)

5 **Highest sand dune:** Great Dune, Cape Henlopen State Park, 80 feet (24 m)

Wilmington is sometimes called the Chemical Capital of the World.

Delaware

Maine

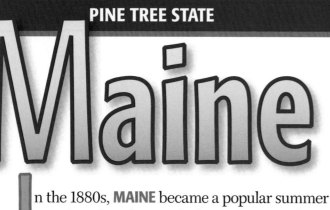

In the 1880s, **MAINE** became a popular summer vacation place for people from Boston and New York. Maine's scenic landscapes still draw people. In the summer, vacationers visit quaint seaside towns like Kennebunk, sail along the rocky coast, enjoy the beaches and gobble down the lobsters for which Maine is famous—about half of the lobsters caught in the U.S. come from Maine waters. The Atlantic coast of Maine is 228 miles (367 km) long, but its tiny bays, islands and inlets make the actual shoreline more than 15 times longer. Farther inland, away from small cities, Maine is a green paradise for hikers, hunters, fishers, paddlers, mountain climbers and wilderness lovers. Maine has more than 2,500 lakes and 5,000 streams, as well as vast forests that cover about 85 percent of the state (a greater percentage than any other state). In winter, people flock to popular ski resorts like Sugarloaf and Saddleback.

In the lower reaches of eastern Maine, farms produce apples, potatoes and dairy products. Maine is also one of the country's main producers of blueberries. Forests cover northern and western Maine, including the rugged White Mountains of the Appalachian chain. Most of these thick forests are owned by lumber companies that make paper and wood products. Whether they stand tall for tourists or are cut down for lumber, Maine's trees are the heart of the state's economy.

THE FACT FILE

Area: 30,865 sq mi
(79,939 sq km)
Population: 1,317,207
Capital: Augusta
Largest cities (with population):
Portland (62,825)
Lewiston (35,234)
Bangor (31,853)
Entered Union (rank):
March 15, 1820 (23)
Motto: *Dirigo* (I lead)
Tree: white pine
Flower: white pinecone
and tassel
Bird: chickadee
Postal code: ME

DID YOU KNOW?

● Maine is the biggest of the New England states—the other five states could almost fit inside its borders.

● West Quoddy Head, Maine, is the easternmost point in the continental U.S.

● Maine is the only state that has just one state bordering it.

● Cadillac Mountain is located on an island off the Maine coast. At 1,530 feet (466 m) high, it is the tallest coastal mountain north of Rio de Janeiro, Brazil.

Katahdin, the name of Maine's tallest peak, is a Penobscot Indian word meaning "greatest mountain."

Bar Harbor can be seen from Cadillac Mountain in Acadia National Park.

CANADA

St. John River

St. John River

Fort Kent
Van Buren

CANADA

Appalachian Mountains

Baxter State Park
▲ Mount Katahdin

Moosehead Lake

Millinocket

Moxie Falls

Penobscot River

Saddleback Ski Resort

▲ Sugarloaf Mountain

Kennebec River

Penobscot Indian Reservation

Angel Falls

Saddleback ▲ Mountain

95

Bangor

West Quoddy Head

Lubec

Androscoggin River

Ocean

Mahoosuc Range

White Mountain National Forest

★ **Augusta**

Bar Harbor
▲ Cadillac Mountain
Acadia National Park

Rockport

Auburn ● Lewiston

Rockland

Atlantic

NEW HAMPSHIRE

Sebago Lake

Yarmouth

Portland ● South Portland

Kennebunk

N
W **TFK** E
S

The breathtaking Angel Falls

0	50	100 mi

0	50	100	150 km

TFK TOP 5

1 **Highest point:** Mount Katahdin, 5,268 feet (1,606 m)

2 **Longest river within state:** Penobscot River, 350 miles (563 km)

3 **Highest waterfalls:** Moxie Falls and Angel Falls (tie), 90 feet (27 m)

4 **Lowest recorded temperature:** -48°F (-44°C), Van Buren, January 19, 1925

5 **Largest lake:** Moosehead Lake, 117 sq mi (303 sq km)

Maine

Maryland

The Chesapeake Bay isn't the geographic center of **MARYLAND**, but it is central to the life and economy of Marylanders. On the eastern side of the 200-mile-long (321 km) bay is the Delmarva Peninsula, named for the three states that form it: DELaware, MARyland and VirginiA. The part of the peninsula belonging to Maryland is called the Eastern Shore of Maryland, and across the waters is the Western Shore. People boat on the bay for pleasure and business. Chesapeake commercial fishermen, known as watermen, harvest a seafood catch bigger than that of any other body of water of the same size. The Western Shore is the location of Baltimore, the state's largest city and one of the nation's major ports. Annapolis, the state capital and home of the U.S. Naval Academy, sits on the Bay to the south of Baltimore.

The Chesapeake Bay and the area around it are part of a low, swampy region called the Coastal Plain. West of the Coastal Plain, the land rises to form the hilly, forested Piedmont region. Still farther west, bordering West Virginia and Virginia, is the Appalachian Plateau. In this rugged region you can find the Allegheny and Blue Ridge Mountains, as well as fertile valleys. This is one of many scenic areas in the state. Maryland has a lot of variety—from mountains to seashore, from big cities to tiny historic towns, from farmers to federal employees. That's why it has been called America in miniature.

THE FACT FILE

Area: 9,775 sq mi (25,316 sq km)
Population: 5,618,344
Capital: Annapolis
Largest cities (with population):
Baltimore (637,455)
Columbia (88,254)
Silver Spring (76,540)
Entered Union (rank):
April 28, 1788 (7)
Motto: *Fatti maschii, parole femine*
(Manly deeds, womanly words)
Tree: white oak
Flower: black-eyed Susan
Bird: Baltimore oriole
Postal code: MD

DID YOU KNOW?

● Smith Island is the only inhabited Maryland island in Chesapeake Bay.

● Baltimore's Inner Harbor is the most popular tourist destination in the city. Among the seaport's attractions are the National Aquarium and the Maryland Science Center.

● Camp David, at Catoctin Mountain Park in the Blue Ridge Mountains, is where the President of the United States has gone to relax since 1942. Presidents entertain visiting heads of state, hold Cabinet meetings and talk to leaders of Congress on its grounds.

Blue crabs from Chesapeake Bay are a Maryland treat.

The Inner Harbor is Baltimore's most popular attraction.

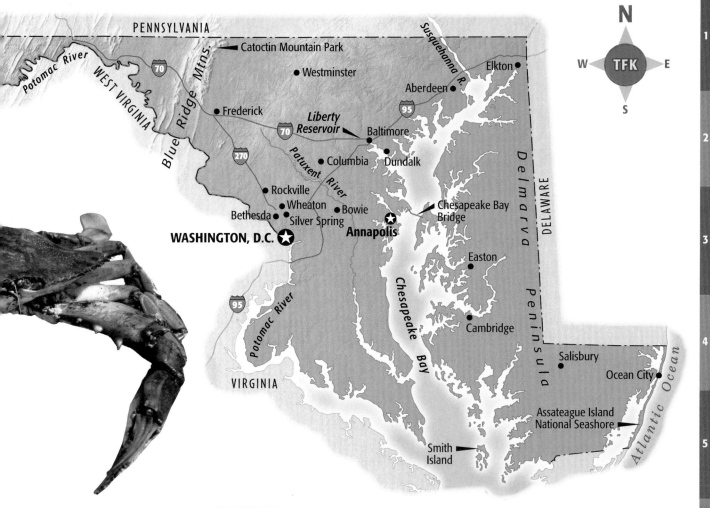

PENNSYLVANIA

Potomac River

WEST VIRGINIA

70

Blue Ridge Mtns.

Catoctin Mountain Park

• Westminster

Susquehanna R.

• Elkton

Aberdeen •

95

• Frederick

Liberty Reservoir

70

Baltimore

270

Patuxent River

• Columbia

Dundalk

Delmarva Peninsula

DELAWARE

• Rockville

• Wheaton

Bethesda • • Silver Spring

• Bowie

Chesapeake Bay Bridge

Annapolis

WASHINGTON, D.C. ★

95

Potomac River

• Easton

Chesapeake Bay

• Cambridge

VIRGINIA

• Salisbury

Ocean City •

Atlantic Ocean

Assateague Island National Seashore

Smith Island

N
W — **TFK** — E
S

100 mi

100   150 km

TFK TOP 5

1 **Highest point:** Backbone Mountain, 3,360 feet (1,025 m)

2 **Longest river within state:** Patuxent River, 110 miles (177 km)

3 **Longest escalator:** 230 feet (70 m), Wheaton Metrorail station, Silver Spring

4 **Longest bridge:** Chesapeake Bay Bridge, 4.3 miles (7 km)

5 **Largest freshwater lake:** Deep Creek Lake, 7 sq mi (18 sq km)

The Chesapeake Bay Bridge connects the Eastern Shore and the Western Shore.

Maryland

Massachusetts

MASSACHUSETTS has played an important part in American history—from the founding of Plymouth Colony and the start of the Revolutionary War to the impact of statesmen like President John F. Kennedy. Even the game of basketball was invented here, in Springfield.

Much of the state's history has been preserved in buildings and landmarks, such as the Paul Revere House in Boston, the Plimoth Plantation in Plymouth and the New Bedford home of Mary and Nathan Johnson, who helped slaves escape to freedom. Tourists come to see those places and others such as Faneuil Hall, in Boston, and the Minute Man National Historical Park, between Lexington and Concord.

Not all the state's attractions are human-made. Scenic green hills and wilderness areas cover the center of the state, in a region called the Coastal Uplands. The lush Connecticut River flows south through the western part of the state. Even farther west, the rural Berkshire Hills are covered by thick forests and etched by rushing streams. In the winter, people come here to ski and snowboard. In the swampy Coastal Lowlands of eastern Massachusetts, tart cranberries grow in bogs. In warm weather, vacationers who have seen enough historical sites head for the islands of Martha's Vineyard and Nantucket to bicycle and relax on the beaches.

THE FACT FILE

Area: 7,838 sq mi (20,300 sq km)
Population: 6,449,755
Capital: Boston
Largest cities (with population):
Boston (599,351)
Worcester (173,966)
Springfield (149,938)
Entered Union (rank):
February 6, 1788 (6)
Motto: *Ense petit placidam sub libertate quietem* (By the sword we seek peace, but peace only under liberty)
Tree: American elm
Flower: mayflower
Bird: chickadee
Postal code: MA

DID YOU KNOW?

● The movie *Jaws* was filmed on Martha's Vineyard.

● The longest name of a place in the U.S. is Lake Chargoggago-ggmanchaugagoggchaubuna-gungamaug, in Webster.

● In the 1930s, Ruth Wakefield invented the chocolate chip cookie at the Toll House Inn, in Whitman. When making chocolate cookies, she ran out of baking chocolate, so she mixed pieces of chocolate into the dough. The chips didn't melt—and the cookie tasted great.

The John Hancock Tower in Boston is the tallest building in New England.

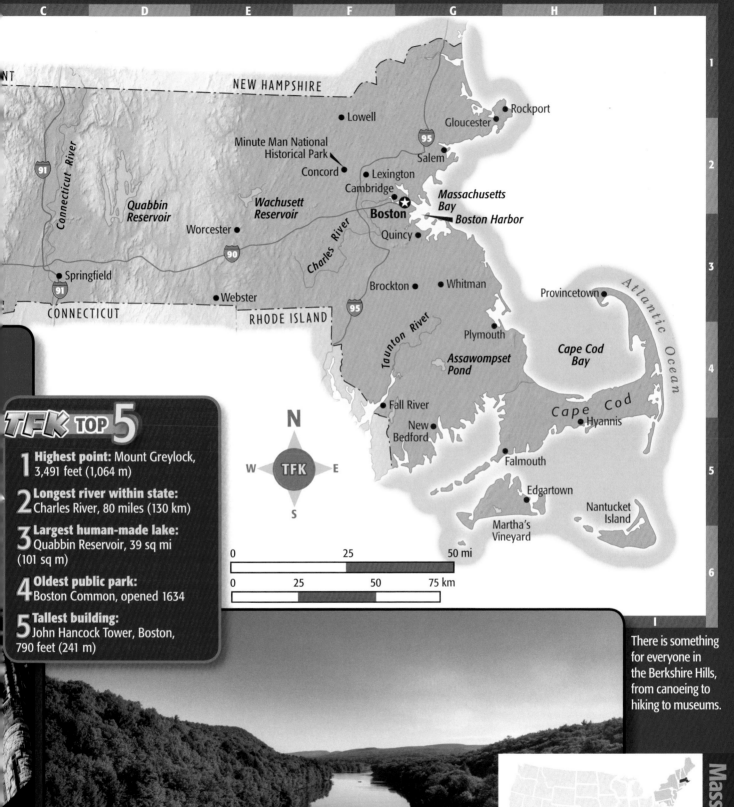

NEW HAMPSHIRE

● Lowell

● Rockport

Gloucester ●

95

Minute Man National
Historical Park

Salem ●

Concord ●

● Lexington

Cambridge ●

Quabbin
Reservoir

Wachusett
Reservoir

Connecticut River

91

★ **Boston**

*Massachusetts
Bay*

Boston Harbor

Worcester ●

Charles River

Quincy ●

90

● Springfield

91

● Webster

CONNECTICUT

RHODE ISLAND

95

Brockton ●

● Whitman

Provincetown ●

Atlantic Ocean

Taunton River

Plymouth ●

*Cape Cod
Bay*

**Assawompset
Pond**

Cape Cod

● Fall River

New ●
Bedford

Hyannis ●

Falmouth ●

Edgartown ●

Nantucket
Island

Martha's
Vineyard

N
W E
TFK
S

| 0 | | 25 | | 50 mi |

| 0 | 25 | 50 | 75 km |

TFK TOP 5

1 **Highest point:** Mount Greylock,
3,491 feet (1,064 m)

2 **Longest river within state:**
Charles River, 80 miles (130 km)

3 **Largest human-made lake:**
Quabbin Reservoir, 39 sq mi
(101 sq m)

4 **Oldest public park:**
Boston Common, opened 1634

5 **Tallest building:**
John Hancock Tower, Boston,
790 feet (241 m)

There is something
for everyone in
the Berkshire Hills,
from canoeing to
hiking to museums.

Massachusetts

New Hampshire

NEW HAMPSHIRE has only 18 miles (29 km) of ocean coastline—the smallest of any U.S. coastal state. Still, its coast is key to much of New Hampshire's history. The first English settlers arrived on the coast, and their towns, including Rye and Portsmouth (both settled in 1623), still stand. New Hampshire's largest cities—and a majority of the state's population—are located within about 50 miles (80 km) of the coast. Most of the state's manufacturing is done in Manchester and nearby cities.

Only about 13 percent of the population lives "up north," as the northern part of the state is called. But this area's spectacular mountains and forests are what draw most visitors. The main attraction in the north is the snow-topped White Mountains. There are 86 peaks in this range, eight of them at least one mile (1.6 km) high. About 65 percent of New Hampshire is covered by forests. Hikers, campers and skiers love the White Mountain National Forest. Each year, its natural beauty draws more visitors than the West's Yellowstone and Yosemite combined. Visitors also enjoy New Hampshire's 1,300 lakes and 40,000 miles (64,360 km) of rivers and streams. A famous rock formation in the White Mountains called Old Man of the Mountain (it was shaped like a man's profile) has long been the state symbol, but in 2003, the Old Man broke apart. Though it collapsed, the rest of the state is going strong.

THE FACT FILE

Area: 8,969 sq mi
(23,231 sq km)
Population: 1,315,828
Capital: Concord
Largest cities (with population):
Manchester (108,874)
Nashua (86,837)
Concord (42,392)
Entered Union (rank):
June 21, 1788 (9)
Motto: Live free or die
Tree: white birch
Flower: purple lilac
Bird: purple finch
Postal code: NH

DID YOU KNOW?

● At age 5, comic Adam Sandler moved to Manchester from Brooklyn, New York. He went to Central High School, where he played hoops and was class clown.

● The town of Keene's annual Pumpkin Festival entered the *Guinness World Records* in 2003 for displaying the most jack-o'-lanterns—28,592.

● The Presidential Range has some of the highest peaks in the White Mountains. They were named for Presidents and statesmen, including Benjamin Franklin and John Adams.

More than 100 waterfalls cascade down the White Mountains.

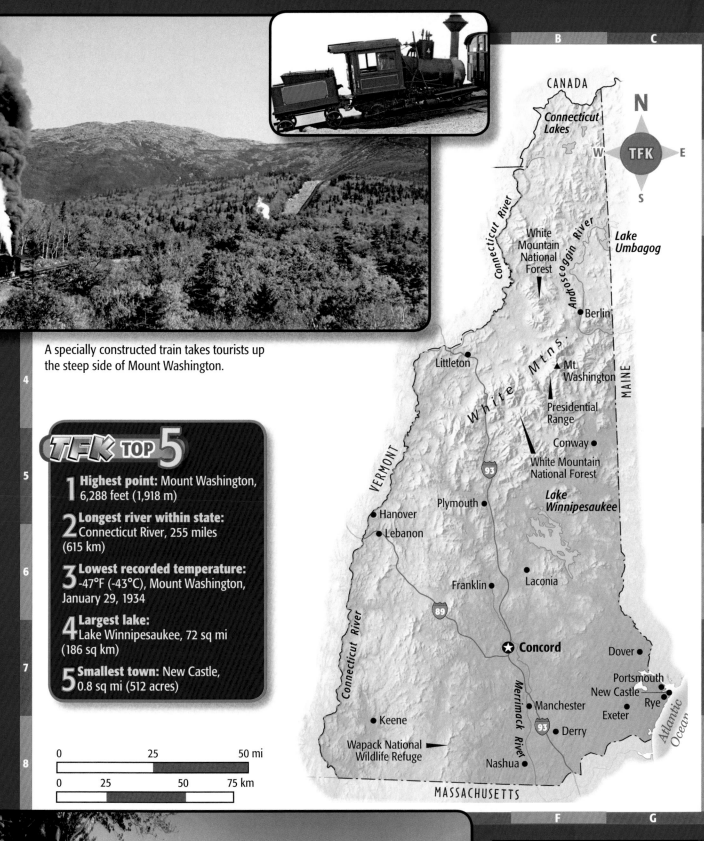

A specially constructed train takes tourists up the steep side of Mount Washington.

TFK TOP 5

1 Highest point: Mount Washington, 6,288 feet (1,918 m)

2 Longest river within state: Connecticut River, 255 miles (615 km)

3 Lowest recorded temperature: -47°F (-43°C), Mount Washington, January 29, 1934

4 Largest lake: Lake Winnipesaukee, 72 sq mi (186 sq km)

5 Smallest town: New Castle, 0.8 sq mi (512 acres)

0   25   50 mi

0   25   50   75 km

CANADA

Connecticut Lakes

N
W — TFK — E
S

White Mountain National Forest

Androscoggin River

Lake Umbagog

Connecticut River

MAINE

Berlin

Littleton

White Mtns.

Mt. Washington

Presidential Range

Conway

White Mountain National Forest

VERMONT

Plymouth

Lake Winnipesaukee

Hanover

Lebanon

Franklin

Laconia

Concord ★

Dover

Portsmouth

New Castle

Rye

Exeter

Manchester

Keene

Derry

Wapack National Wildlife Refuge

Merrimack River

Nashua

Atlantic Ocean

MASSACHUSETTS

Lake Winnipesaukee is 21 miles (34 km) long and contains hundreds of small islands.

New Jersey

Founded in 1746, Princeton University is one of the eight Ivy League universities.

NEW JERSEY is nicknamed the Garden State for good reason. It is a green state, where nearly 9,000 farms take up about 10 percent of the land. Most of the farms are in the southern Coastal Plain, which makes up more than half the state. They provide fresh fruit and vegetables, as well as dairy products, to many eastern states. Along the Atlantic Coast is the Jersey Shore, an area of sandy beaches lined with pretty resort towns like Cape May. Southern New Jersey contains one of the nation's most amazing undeveloped areas, the New Jersey Pine Barrens. A National Reserve, with 1,718 sq mi (4,449 sq km) of pine forests, it was named a United Nations International Biosphere Reserve in 1983.

New Jersey is also an industrial state. It has about 15,000 factories and many oil refineries. New Jersey has some large cities, such as Newark and Jersey City, many of them within commuting distance of New York City. But the Garden State also has mountain ranges, rushing rivers, waterfalls, gorges, lakes and the dramatic Palisades cliffs that rise up from the Hudson River. That's why, of all the industries in New Jersey, tourism is the second largest.

THE FACT FILE

Area: 7,813 sq mi (20,236 sq km)
Population: 8,685,920
Capital: Trenton
Largest cities (with population):
Newark (280,135)
Jersey City (242,389)
Paterson (146,545)
Entered Union (rank):
December 18, 1787 (3)
Motto: Liberty and prosperity
Tree: red oak
Flower: violet
Bird: eastern goldfinch
Postal code: NJ

DID YOU KNOW?

● On March 31, 1870, Thomas Mundy Peterson, of Perth Amboy, became the first African American to vote in a U.S. election. He did it after the 15th Amendment was ratified, which gave all American males the right to vote.

● About 90 percent of people in New Jersey live in urban areas, the highest percentage of urban population of any U.S. state.

● Marvin Gardens, Oriental Avenue, Park Place and the rest of the properties in the game of Monopoly are named after streets in or near Atlantic City. The game's designer, Charles Darrow, lived in Atlantic City in the summer.

The Delaware Water Gap cuts through a mountain ridge separating New Jersey and Pennsylvania.

TFK TOP 5

1 **Highest point:** High Point, 1,803 feet (550 m)

2 **Longest river within state:** Passaic River, 80 miles (130 km)

3 **Biggest natural lake within state:** Lake Hopatcong, 4.2 sq mi (10 sq km)

4 **Highest waterfall:** Great Falls, 77 feet (23 m)

5 **Tallest building:** Goldman Sachs Tower, Jersey City, 781 feet (238 m)

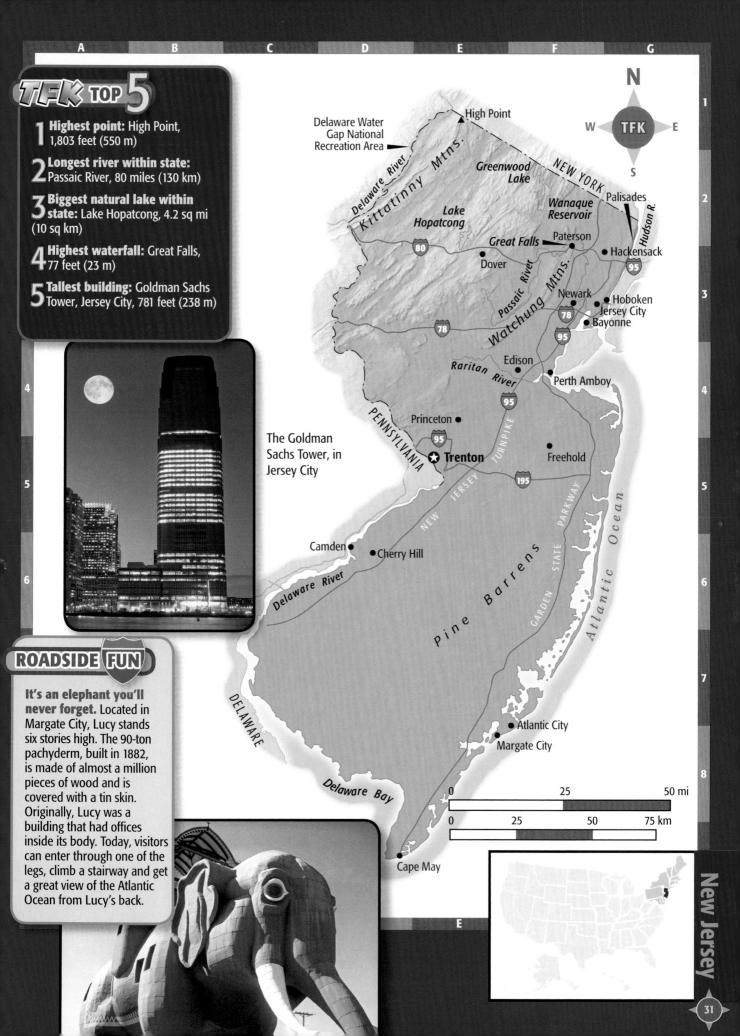

The Goldman Sachs Tower, in Jersey City

ROADSIDE FUN

It's an elephant you'll never forget. Located in Margate City, Lucy stands six stories high. The 90-ton pachyderm, built in 1882, is made of almost a million pieces of wood and is covered with a tin skin. Originally, Lucy was a building that had offices inside its body. Today, visitors can enter through one of the legs, climb a stairway and get a great view of the Atlantic Ocean from Lucy's back.

Delaware Water Gap National Recreation Area

High Point

N
W TFK E
S

NEW YORK

Greenwood Lake

Kittatinny Mtns.

Delaware River

Lake Hopatcong

Wanaque Reservoir

Palisades

Hudson R.

Great Falls

Paterson

Hackensack

80

Dover

Passaic River

Watchung Mtns.

Newark

Hoboken
Jersey City

78

Bayonne

95

78

Edison

Raritan River

Perth Amboy

95

Princeton

95

PENNSYLVANIA

Trenton

Freehold

NEW JERSEY TURNPIKE

195

GARDEN STATE PARKWAY

Atlantic Ocean

Camden

Cherry Hill

Delaware River

Pine Barrens

DELAWARE

Atlantic City

Margate City

Delaware Bay

Cape May

0   25   50 mi

0   25   50   75 km

New Jersey

New York

Adirondack Park is about as big as the combined areas of Yellowstone, Yosemite, Grand Canyon, Glacier and Great Smoky Mountains national parks.

Often when residents of the Empire State say "New York," they mean New York City. But **NEW YORK** State is much more than "the City." It has scenic mountains, such as the Catskills in the south and the Adirondacks in the north. At 9,375 sq mi (24,281 sq km), Adirondack Park is the largest state park in the contiguous U.S. New York has more than 6,700 reservoirs and lakes, including Lake Champlain in the northeast and the Finger Lakes in the west. Lake Erie, on the state's western border, flows into Lake Ontario, forming Niagara Falls. In the Hudson River Valley, which is in the eastern part of the state, charming small towns and grand mansions sit amid scenic splendor. Farms in the north and just south of the Great Lakes produce all types of fruits and vegetables and are among the nation's leaders in dairy products. Commercial fishermen catch a large variety of seafood off the waters of Long Island.

Of course, it's hard to ignore the importance of New York City. It is the nation's largest city, with the second-largest economy of any city in the world. It is a leader in manufacturing, foreign trade, commerce and banking, publishing, fashion, art and theater. It is a top seaport, has one of the world's busiest airports and is home to the New York Stock Exchange, not to mention the Statue of Liberty.

THE FACT FILE

Area: 53,097 sq mi (137,521 sq km)
Population: 19,297,729
Capital: Albany
Largest cities (with population):
New York City (8,274,527)
Buffalo (272,632)
Rochester (206,759)
Entered Union (rank):
July 26, 1788 (11)
Motto: *Excelsior* (Ever upward)
Tree: sugar maple
Flower: rose
Bird: bluebird
Postal code: NY

DID YOU KNOW?

● The Federal Reserve Bank in New York City stores more than 25 percent of the world's gold reserves in a vault 80 feet (24 m) below street level.

● In August 1969, the Woodstock Festival, the most famous rock concert in history, took place in a field in Bethel, New York, before an audience of nearly half a million people.

● Buffalo wings, fried chicken wings that are coated in hot sauce, were first served in the city of Buffalo. In Buffalo, however, the snack is usually offered with a blue cheese dressing and called simply "wings."

Niagara Falls
Buffalo
90
Lake Erie
Allegheny River
E
3
4
5

The Empire State Building is lit up for Christmas.

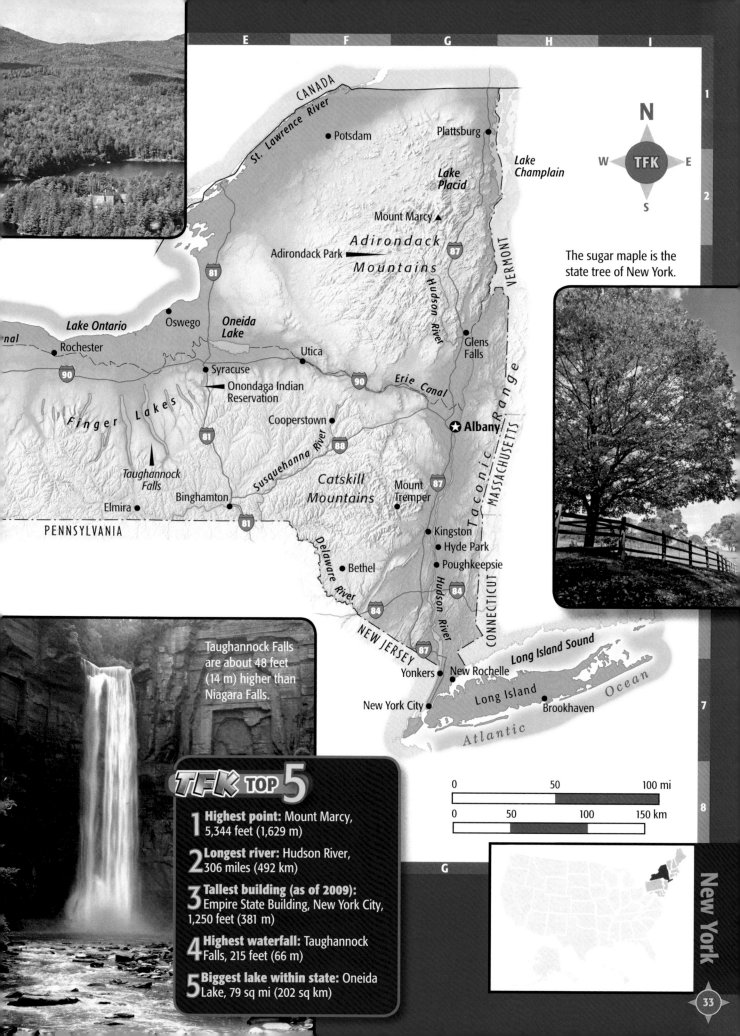

N
W — **TFK** — E
S

CANADA

St. Lawrence River

• Potsdam   Plattsburg •

Lake Placid

Lake Champlain

Mount Marcy ▲

Adirondack

Adirondack Park ►   *Mountains*

87

VERMONT

The sugar maple is the state tree of New York.

Hudson River

Lake Ontario   Oswego •   *Oneida Lake*

• Rochester   Utica •   Glens Falls

90   Syracuse •

                Onondaga Indian Reservation

Erie Canal   90

Finger Lakes   Cooperstown •   ★ **Albany**

81

Taghannock Falls   88

                Susquehanna River

• Elmira   Binghamton •   *Catskill Mountains*   Mount Tremper •

PENNSYLVANIA   81   87

                                Kingston •
                                Hyde Park •
                Delaware River   Poughkeepsie •

                • Bethel   Hudson River   84

84   NEW JERSEY   87

Taghannock Falls are about 48 feet (14 m) higher than Niagara Falls.

Long Island Sound

Yonkers • New Rochelle •

New York City •   Long Island   Brookhaven •

Atlantic   Ocean

TACONIC RANGE
MASSACHUSETTS
CONNECTICUT

0 ——— 50 ——— 100 mi
0 — 50 — 100 — 150 km

TFK TOP 5

1 Highest point: Mount Marcy, 5,344 feet (1,629 m)

2 Longest river: Hudson River, 306 miles (492 km)

3 Tallest building (as of 2009): Empire State Building, New York City, 1,250 feet (381 m)

4 Highest waterfall: Taghannock Falls, 215 feet (66 m)

5 Biggest lake within state: Oneida Lake, 79 sq mi (202 sq km)

New York

Pennsylvania

Y ou can find Independence Hall, the Liberty Bell, Valley Forge and the Gettysburg battlefield in **PENNSYLVANIA**. You can also find—and eat—plenty of pretzels, a tasty treat that was made popular in the U.S. by Pennsylvanians. Pennsylvania's historic sites bring tourists, but food is nearly as important to its economy. In addition to pretzels, the state is a leader in the production of potato chips, chocolate snacks, ketchup, ice cream and bread. It is also a major manufacturer of medicines, electronics and chemical products. Pennsylvania is the fourth largest producer of coal in the U.S. The state makes steel products (that's how the Pittsburgh Steelers football team got its name), but not as much as it once did.

Two large metropolitan areas, Pittsburgh and Philadelphia, sit at opposite ends of the state. But about one-third of Pennsylvania is rural. The southeast is gently rolling countryside, containing many of the state's nearly 60,000 farms. Much of the richest farmland is owned by the Amish, a religious group that lives without modern conveniences. Toward the west is a series of ridges and valleys that includes the Blue Ridge Mountains and the Great Appalachian Valley. The Appalachian Plateau covers the northern and western parts of the state. Here the Allegheny Mountains draw people to their lush forests and nature trails.

THE FACT FILE

Area: 46,056 sq mi (119,284 sq km)
Population: 12,432,792
Capital: Harrisburg
Largest cities (with population):
Philadelphia (1,449,634)
Pittsburgh (311,218)
Allentown (107,117)
Entered Union (rank):
December 12, 1787 (2)
Motto: Virtue, liberty and independence
Tree: hemlock
Flower: mountain laurel
Bird: ruffed grouse
Postal code: PA

DID YOU KNOW?

● Every August since 1947, the Little League World Series has been played in Williamsport. Kids ages 11 to 13 from all across the world take part in the baseball tournament.

● The world's first commercial oil well was drilled at Titusville, in northwestern Pennsylvania, in 1859.

● The town of Hershey is the home of the Hershey Company, a candymaker that makes more than 80 million chocolate kisses a day at its factories here and in Virginia. Even the streetlights in Hershey are in the shape of kisses.

The Allegheny National Forest is a popular recreation place.

Map labels:
Lake Erie
Titusville
Pymatuning Reservoir
Allegheny River
New Castle
Pittsburgh
Ohio River
Monongahela River
Laurel Caverns
OHIO
WEST VIRGINIA
Appalach

0   50   100 mi

0   50   100   150 km

N
W TFK E
S

NEW YORK

← Allegheny National Forest

Plateau

Mountains

81

Scranton

Lake Wallenpaupack

Williamsport

Wilkes-Barre

80

80

Delaware River

• Punxsutawney

Mountains

Susquehanna River

81

Mountains

Bethlehem

Allentown

78

NEW JERSEY

Altoona

Johnstown

Allegheny

Raystown Lake

Appalachian

Schuylkill River

Delaware River

Reading

Harrisburg ☆

• Hershey

76

Great Appalachian Valley

76

Phoenixville

Valley Forge

76

70

81

Blue Ridge Mtns.

• Lancaster

Philadelphia

70

Chester

▲ Mount Davis

Gettysburg

DE.

MARYLAND

ROADSIDE FUN

If you happen to be in the town of Punxsutawney on Groundhog Day, you are in for a treat. Every February 2, a special ceremony is held just outside of town at Gobblers Knob. With much fanfare, Punxsutawney Phil, a real groundhog, is brought out of his burrow. Tradition has it that if Phil sees his shadow and scurries back to his hole, there will be six more weeks of winter. If he doesn't see his shadow, spring will come soon. According to people in Punxsutawney, Phil's predictions are never wrong.

The U.S. Declaration of Independence and the Constitution were signed at Independence Hall in Philadelphia.

TFK TOP 5

1 **Highest point:** Mount Davis, 3,213 feet (980 m)

2 **Highest recorded temperature:** 111°F (43°C), Phoenixville, July 10, 1936

3 **Largest human-made lake:** Pymatuning Reservoir (partly in Ohio), 26 sq mi (67 sq km)

4 **Tallest building:** Comcast Center, Philadelphia, 975 feet (297 m)

5 **Largest cave:** Laurel Caverns, 2.8 miles (4.5 km) long

Rhode Island

RHODE ISLAND is the nation's smallest state in area. It's so small, it takes less than an hour to drive from border to border. A lot of people are packed into this small space: Rhode Island is the second most densely populated state, with 1,012 people per square mile. About 90 percent of the population lives in cities. In the 1800s, these cities and towns used natural waterpower to manufacture cotton yarn and textiles, making Rhode Island an industrial giant. It still is. Jewelry, silverware, plastics, electronics, boats and ships are manufactured here. Many people also work for the state government and at U.S. naval facilities. The western half of Rhode Island is more rural than the eastern half. This is part of the New England Upland, a rocky region that doesn't have much farmland. Next to Alaska, the amount of income Rhode Island produces from agriculture is the least in the U.S.

Lots of people visit this little state. The biggest draw is the resorts along the coast, where people come to sail, fish and eat the famous quahog clams. Narragansett Bay has more than 30 islands, some large enough to hold towns. Located about 12 miles (21 km) off the mainland is Block Island, where vacationers bike and hike through a rustic landscape and past historic lighthouses. Newport, on the island of Aquidneck (also known as Rhode Island), is a town of beautiful harbors and beaches. It's also where, in the 1800s, some of the nation's wealthiest people built mansions to serve as summer homes. Today, tourists can get a glimpse of what life was like for the super-rich in an era called the Gilded Age.

THE FACT FILE

Area: 1,045 sq mi
(2,706 sq km)
Population: 1,057,832
Capital: Providence
Largest cities (with population):
Providence (172,459)
Warwick (85,097)
Cranston (80,463)
Entered Union (rank):
May 29, 1790 (13)
Motto: hope
Tree: red maple
Flower: violet
Bird: Rhode Island Red chicken
Postal code: RI

DID YOU KNOW?

● Rhode Island (Aquidneck) may have gotten its name from an explorer who saw the red soil of Aquidneck Island and named it Roodt Eylandt—Dutch for "red island."

● One of the favorite drinks of Rhode Islanders is coffee milk—coffee syrup stirred into milk.

● The longest professional baseball game took place in Pawtucket. In 1981, two minor league teams, the Pawtucket Red Sox and the Rochester Red Wings, played a game that went 33 innings and took 8 hours 25 minutes to complete.

The Breakers was the Newport summer home of a Vanderbilt family member.

The Providence River runs through the city of Providence.

On Block Island, people bike and hike through a rustic landscape and past historic lighthouses.

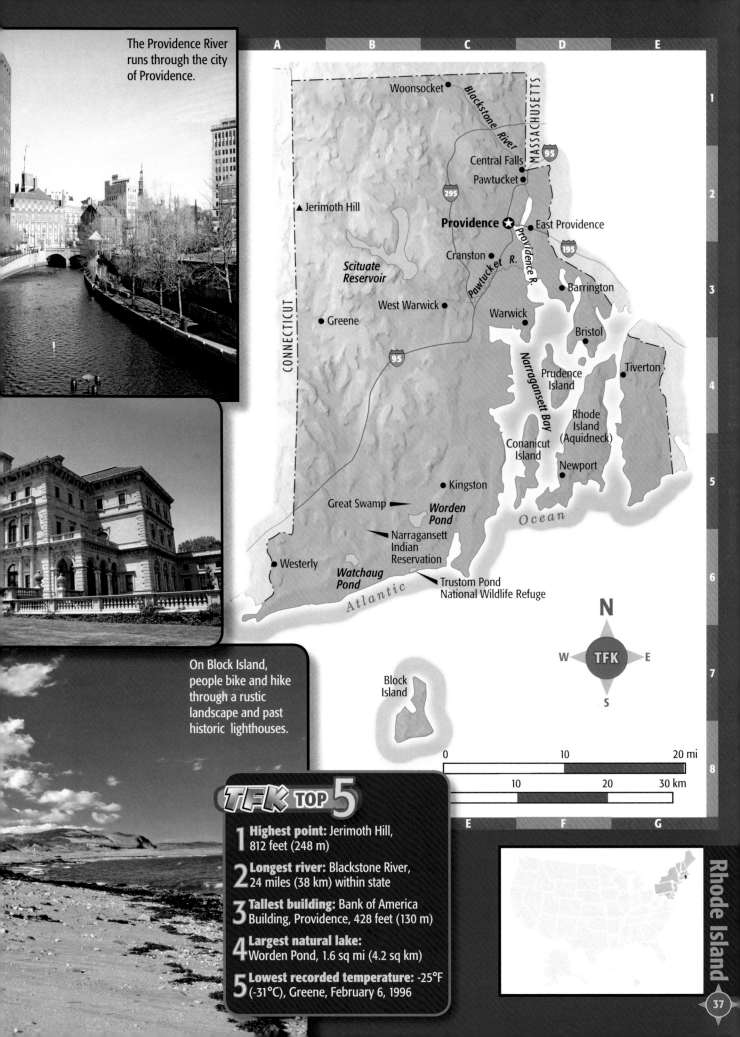

Woonsocket

Blackstone River

MASSACHUSETTS

Central Falls
Pawtucket

▲ Jerimoth Hill

Providence ☆

East Providence

Cranston

Providence R.

Pawtucket R.

Scituate Reservoir

Barrington

West Warwick

Warwick

Bristol

CONNECTICUT

Greene

Tiverton

Prudence Island

Narragansett Bay

Rhode Island (Aquidneck)

Conanicut Island

Newport

Kingston

Great Swamp

Worden Pond

Ocean

Narragansett Indian Reservation

Westerly

Watchaug Pond

Trustom Pond National Wildlife Refuge

Atlantic

Block Island

N
W TFK E
S

0   10   20 mi

10   20   30 km

TFK TOP 5

1 Highest point: Jerimoth Hill, 812 feet (248 m)

2 Longest river: Blackstone River, 24 miles (38 km) within state

3 Tallest building: Bank of America Building, Providence, 428 feet (130 m)

4 Largest natural lake: Worden Pond, 1.6 sq mi (4.2 sq km)

5 Lowest recorded temperature: -25°F (-31°C), Greene, February 6, 1996

Rhode Island

Vermont

VERMONT is a winter wonderland. People love to ski and snowboard on such mountains as Killington Peak and Stratton Mountain. Vermont is also an autumn wonderland, when the leaves on millions of trees change colors, drawing "leaf peepers," as Vermonters call fall tourists. Spring and summer aren't bad, either: Three-quarters of the state is covered by trees, and people hike and camp in Vermont's 52 state parks, two national parks and the Green Mountain National Forest. All year round, tourists visit Vermont's picturesque little towns.

Vermont is one of the nation's smallest states, only 89 miles (143 km) at its widest point. It's not hard for the Green Mountains, which run the length of the state, to stand out here. West of the Green Mountains is the Champlain Valley. South and east of the Green Mountains is the New England Upland region, where the land slopes down until it reaches the narrow valley made by the Connecticut River.

Vermont may be more famous for its cheddar cheese than its mountains. There are plenty of dairy farms, also producing milk and butter. Vermont is No.1 in maple syrup, producing almost one-third of the nation's supply. It goes well with the large amounts of ice cream made from Vermont milk.

THE FACT FILE

Area: 9,249 sq mi
(23,956 sq km)
Population: 621,254
Capital: Montpelier
Largest cities (with population):
Burlington (38,531)
South Burlington (17,445)
Rutland (16,826)
Entered Union (rank):
March 4, 1791 (14)
Motto: Freedom and unity
Tree: sugar maple
Flower: red clover
Bird: hermit thrush
Postal code: VT

DID YOU KNOW?

● With a population of 7,806, Montpelier is the least populous state capital in the U.S.

● In 1978, childhood friends Ben Cohen and Jerry Greenfield opened an ice cream shop in Burlington. Today, Ben & Jerry's ice cream is world famous.

● On July 8, 1777, Vermont created an independent republic and adopted a constitution that abolished slavery. Vermont didn't become a U.S. state until 1791, so it was a sovereign nation when it ended slavery—the first modern country to do so.

Tourists head to Vermont in the fall, when the trees turn amazing colors.

The peaks around Killington attract the most skiers in eastern North America.

CANADA

| | A | B | C | D | E |

Seymour Lake

Canaan

• St. Albans

Bloomfield

91

Granby •

• Burlington

▲ Mount Mansfield

• Stowe

St. Johnsbury •

South Burlington

Waterbury

93

Lake Champlain

☆ **Montpelier**

89 • Barre

Otter Creek

Green Mountain National Forest

91

Salisbury

Leicester •

Lake Bomoseen

White River

Rutland •

▲ Killington Peak

NEW YORK

NEW HAMPSHIRE

Connecticut River

Taconic Mountains

Green Mountains

Appalachian Mountains

Green Mountain National Forest

Stratton Mt. ▲

West Dummerston •

91

• Bennington

Brattleboro •

Mount Snow ▲

MASSACHUSETTS

N
W — TFK — E
S

| 0 | 25 | 50 mi |
| 0 | 25 | 50 | 75 km |

TFK TOP 5

1 **Highest point:** Mount Mansfield, 4,393 feet (1,340 m)

2 **Longest covered bridge open to traffic:** in West Dummerston, 271 feet (82 m)

3 **Longest river within state:** Otter Creek, 100 miles (160 km)

4 **Lowest recorded temperature:** -50°F (-45°C), Bloomfield, December 30, 1933

5 **Largest lake within state:** Lake Bomoseen, 3 sq mi (9 sq km)

Vermont

South

Martin Luther King, Jr. was born in Atlanta, Georgia.

For much of its history, the South's economy has depended on cotton. Today, cotton may no longer be king in the South, but agriculture is still a major part of the region's economy. Rice and soybeans are major crops, as is poultry production. But as more people move to cities, industry has become more important to the South's economy. Auto-parts manufacturing, communications, textiles and electronics are some of the big industries of the region. Many large corporations, such as The Home Depot, Bank of America and the Fedex Corporation, have headquarters in the South.

The Civil Rights movement began in the 1960s in the South, which became the scene of many demonstrations. The protests led to an end to segregation.

Nowadays, people appreciate the South as a region of great beauty, with landscapes ranging from high mountains, such as the vast Great Smoky Mountains in Tennessee and North Carolina, to vast national forests like the Ouachita National Forest in Arkansas, to coastal wetlands, like the ones that stretch across southern Louisiana.

They also enjoy its slow-moving way of life, where good manners and hospitality are valued and where history comes alive in its towns and historic sites.

THE FACT FILE

States: Alabama, Arkansas, Florida, Georgia, Kentucky, Louisiana, Mississippi, North Carolina, South Carolina, Tennessee, Virginia, West Virginia
Area: 528,837 sq mi (1,369,682 sq km)
Population: 75,861,690
Highest point: Mount Mitchell, North Carolina, 6,684 feet (2,037 m)
Lowest point: New Orleans, Louisiana, 8 feet (2 m) below sea level
Largest state: Georgia: 57,919 sq mi (150,009 sq km)
Smallest state: West Virginia: 24,087 sq mi (62,384 sq km)
Most populous state: Florida, 18,251,243
Least populous state: West Virginia, 1,812,035

DID YOU KNOW?

● The Florida Keys are islands that stretch 192 miles (309 km). The city of Key West on the island of Key West is the southernmost city in the continental U.S.

● The city of Texarkana is in both Arkansas and Texas: the state line goes right down the middle of the city. Each side of the border has its own mayor and police department.

● In 1870, North Carolinian Hiram Rhoades Revels became the first African American to be elected to the U.S. Congress, as Mississippi Senator.

Kentucky is famous for its many horse farms.

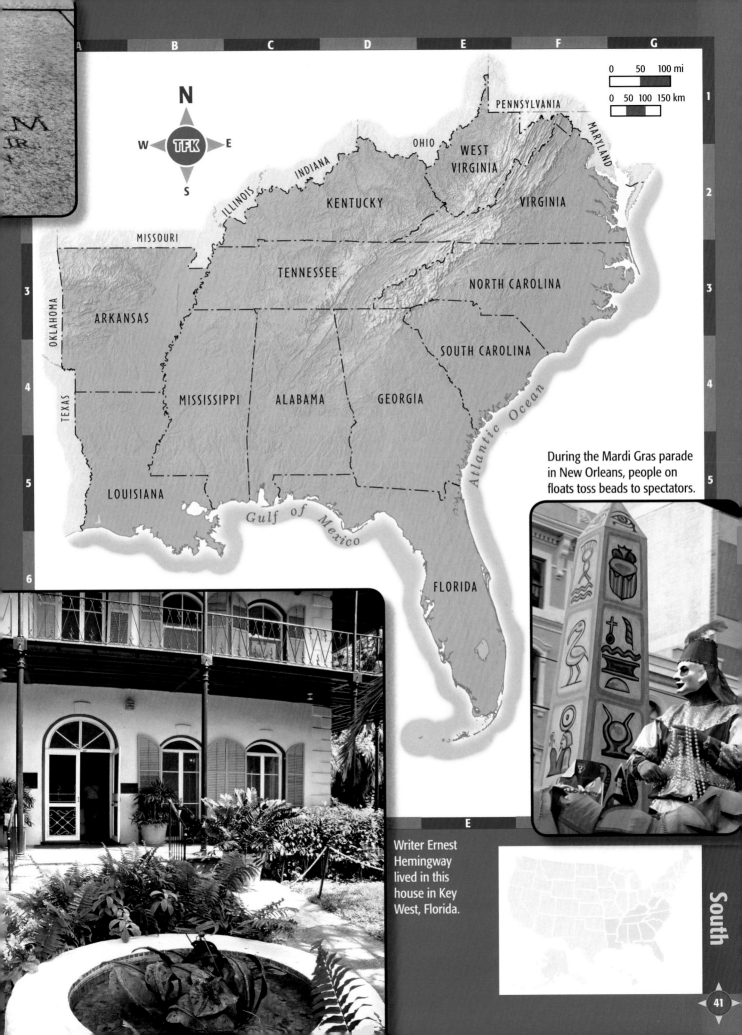

0   50   100 mi

0   50   100 150 km

N

W — TFK — E

S

PENNSYLVANIA

OHIO

WEST VIRGINIA

MARYLAND

INDIANA

ILLINOIS

KENTUCKY

VIRGINIA

MISSOURI

TENNESSEE

NORTH CAROLINA

OKLAHOMA

ARKANSAS

SOUTH CAROLINA

TEXAS

MISSISSIPPI   ALABAMA   GEORGIA

Atlantic Ocean

LOUISIANA

Gulf of Mexico

FLORIDA

During the Mardi Gras parade in New Orleans, people on floats toss beads to spectators.

Writer Ernest Hemingway lived in this house in Key West, Florida.

South

Alabama

UNTIL JUSTICE ROLLS DOWN LIK
AND RIGHTEOUSNESS LIKE A MIGH

MAR

O f all the states, **ALABAMA** has the greatest percentage of people who were born in the state and still live there. So it's no wonder Alabamans honor their heritage—and their history of overcoming tough times. Cotton was the engine of their economy until 1915, when an insect called the boll weevil destroyed most of the cotton crop. But farmers were able to replace cotton with peanuts (Alabama is the No. 3 state in peanut production). Alabamans also earn income by raising cattle and poultry in the farmlands of the Eastern Coastal Plains, which cover much of central and south Alabama. The civil rights movement was also born in this state. In 1955, Martin Luther King, Jr. helped end official segregation in Alabama by leading the Montgomery bus boycott.

Alabama is filled with natural charm. The state has a warm climate, rich soil and endless rivers and lakes—most formed by dams. Two-thirds of the state is covered by woodlands, and there is a huge variety of animals and plants in its four national forests, like Talladega, and 22 state parks, like DeSoto State Park, which has the deepest canyons east of the Mississippi River. To go even deeper, people explore Russell Cave and other caverns in the state's northeast.

THE FACT FILE

Area: 50,744 sq mi (131,427 sq km)

Population: 4,627,851

Capital: Montgomery

Largest cities (with population):
Birmingham (229,800)
Montgomery (204,086)
Mobile (191,411)

Entered Union (rank):
December 14, 1819 (22)

Motto: *Audemus jura nostra defendere* (We dare defend our rights)

Tree: southern longleaf pine

Flower: camellia

Bird: yellowhammer (yellow-shafted flicker)

Postal code: AL

DID YOU KNOW?

● Huntsville is home to Space Camp, where kids can train like astronauts on simulators and experience what it is like to go on space missions.

● Harper Lee, from Monroeville, wrote *To Kill a Mockingbird*, a famous novel about racial injustice in a small Alabama town.

● About half of all peanuts grown in the U.S. come from within a 100-mile (160 km) radius of the town of Dothan.

Montgomery became Alabama's capital in 1846. It was also the capital of the Confederacy, in 1861.

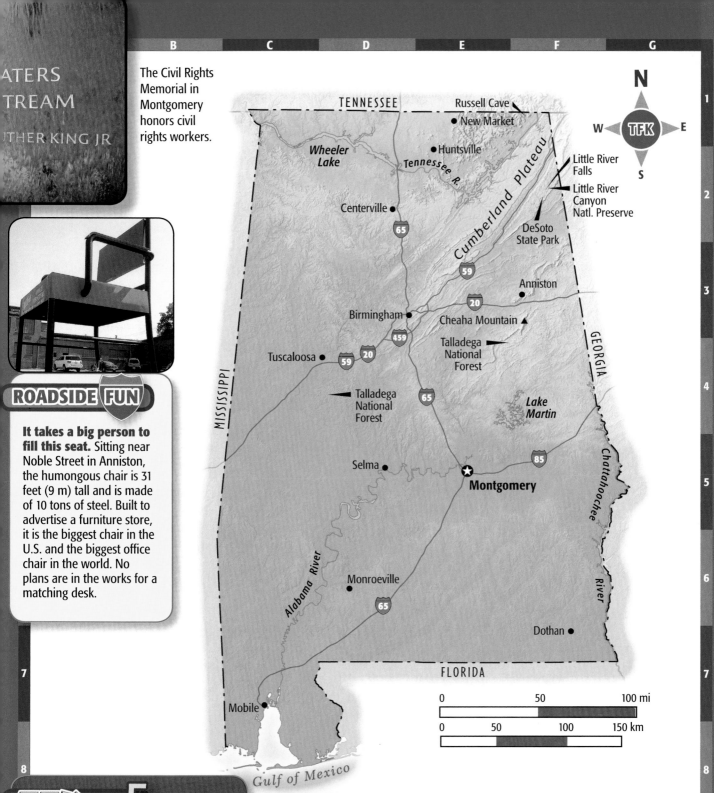

ATERS
TREAM
THER KING JR

The Civil Rights Memorial in Montgomery honors civil rights workers.

N
W — TFK — E
S

TENNESSEE

Russell Cave
New Market
Huntsville

Wheeler Lake

Tennessee R.

Cumberland Plateau

Little River Falls

Little River Canyon Natl. Preserve

Centerville

65

DeSoto State Park

59

Anniston

20

Birmingham

Cheaha Mountain ▲

459

Talladega National Forest

GEORGIA

Tuscaloosa

59   20

65

Talladega National Forest

Lake Martin

Selma

85

★ **Montgomery**

Chattahoochee River

MISSISSIPPI

Alabama River

Monroeville

65

Dothan

FLORIDA

0   50   100 mi
0   50   100   150 km

Mobile

Gulf of Mexico

ROADSIDE FUN

It takes a big person to fill this seat. Sitting near Noble Street in Anniston, the humongous chair is 31 feet (9 m) tall and is made of 10 tons of steel. Built to advertise a furniture store, it is the biggest chair in the U.S. and the biggest office chair in the world. No plans are in the works for a matching desk.

TFK TOP 5

1 **Highest point:** Cheaha Mountain, 2,405 feet (733 m)

2 **Tallest building:** RSA Battle House Tower, Mobile, 745 feet (227 m)

3 **Highest recorded temperature:** 112°F (44°C), Centerville, September 5, 1925

4 **Lowest recorded temperature:** -27°F (-32°C), New Market, January 30, 1966

5 **Deepest canyon:** Little River Canyon, 600 feet (182 m)

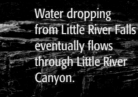

Water dropping from Little River Falls eventually flows through Little River Canyon.

Alabama

NATURAL STATE

Arkansas

Little Rock's Capitol Building is a copy of the U.S. Capitol.

Take a map of **ARKANSAS** and draw a diagonal line from northeast to southwest. Most of the land above the line is mountainous: the rugged Boston and Ouachita mountains are here. Below the line is low country—plains, hills, pine forests and swamps along the southern reaches of the Mississippi River. At its center, the line cuts through Little Rock, the state capital.

About 22 percent of Arkansas land is used for agriculture, especially for growing rice (it produces more than any other state). Cotton is grown in the east, near the Mississippi River in an area called the Delta. But Arkansas's most profitable product is chickens. The state is the leading poultry producer in the U.S. It supplies more than 12 percent of the country's eggs, chickens and turkeys. One out of every 12 jobs in the state is in the poultry industry.

Arkansas is a rural state, with few really large cities and a lot of unspoiled land. It has huge state parks for hikers, mountains for climbers and many caves for spelunkers (cave explorers). After an active day in the outdoors, people can visit the city (and national park) of Hot Springs. It has 47 natural hot springs, and many people come here to bathe in these relaxing—and some say healthful—waters.

THE FACT FILE

Area: 52,075 sq mi (134,874 sq km)

Population: 2,834,797

Capital: Little Rock

Largest cities (with population):
Little Rock (187,452)
Fort Smith (84,375)
Fayetteville (72,208)

Entered Union (rank):
June 15, 1836 (25)

Motto: *Regnat populus*
(The people rule)

Tree: pine

Flower: apple blossom

Bird: mockingbird

Postal code: AR

DID YOU KNOW?

● Crater of Diamonds State Park in Murfreesboro is the only active diamond mine in the U.S. Visitors are allowed to keep any gems they find.

● From December 1811 to January 1812, Arkansas was the epicenter of several earthquakes that were so powerful they formed new lakes and changed the path of the Mississippi River.

● Arkansas has more bauxite than any other state. Bauxite contains aluminum, the metal used to make soda cans.

The average temperature of the thermal waters in Hot Springs National Park is 143°F (62°C).

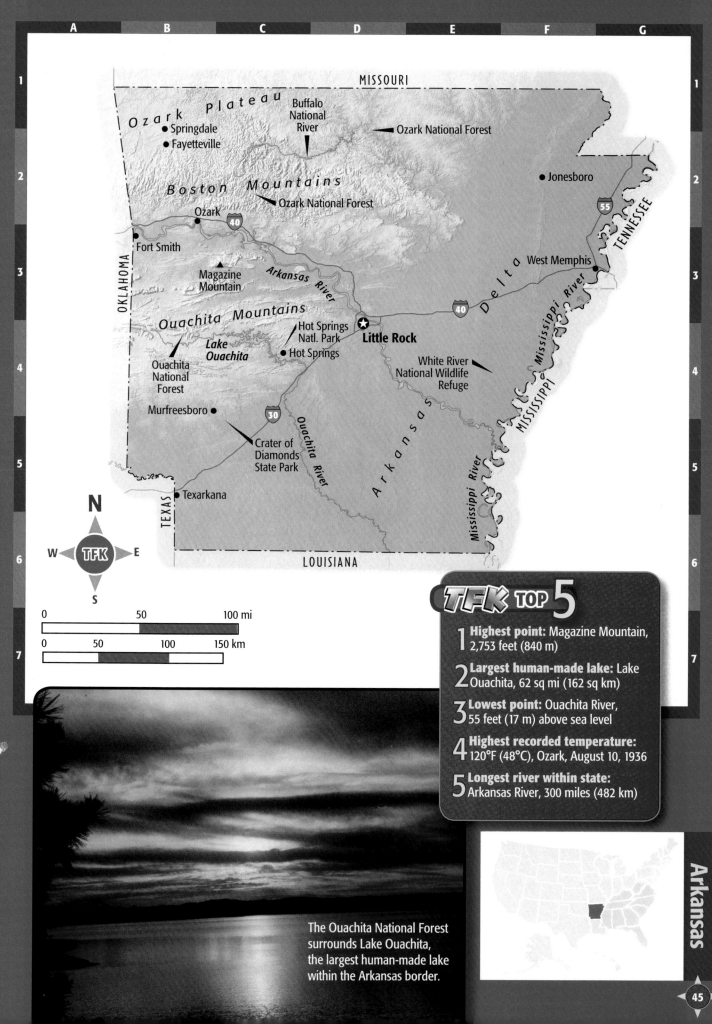

MISSOURI

A B C D E F G

Ozark Plateau

• Springdale
• Fayetteville

Buffalo National River

➤ Ozark National Forest

Boston Mountains

➤ Ozark National Forest

• Ozark
40

• Jonesboro

55

Fort Smith

OKLAHOMA

▲ Magazine Mountain

Arkansas River

Delta

West Memphis •

Mississippi River

TENNESSEE

Ouachita Mountains

Hot Springs Natl. Park

40

Lake Ouachita

• Hot Springs

Little Rock ★

Ouachita National Forest

White River National Wildlife Refuge ➤

• Murfreesboro

30

Ouachita River

Arkansas

Mississippi River

MISSISSIPPI

Crater of Diamonds State Park

• Texarkana

TEXAS

Mississippi River

LOUISIANA

N
W ⟵ TFK ⟶ E
S

0   50   100 mi

0   50   100   150 km

TFK TOP 5

1 Highest point: Magazine Mountain, 2,753 feet (840 m)

2 Largest human-made lake: Lake Ouachita, 62 sq mi (162 sq km)

3 Lowest point: Ouachita River, 55 feet (17 m) above sea level

4 Highest recorded temperature: 120°F (48°C), Ozark, August 10, 1936

5 Longest river within state: Arkansas River, 300 miles (482 km)

The Ouachita National Forest surrounds Lake Ouachita, the largest human-made lake within the Arkansas border.

Arkansas

SUNSHINE STATE

Florida

Florida has 663 miles (1,067 km) of beaches.

FLORIDA is one of the top tourist destinations in the world. Millions of people arrive every year to enjoy its warm weather and more than 600 miles (965 km) of beaches. Except for an area in the northwest called the Panhandle, Florida is a peninsula, and it has more coastline than any state except Alaska. About 75 percent of the state's population lives along the coast.

Florida offers many attractions for visitors, including Walt Disney World in Orlando, the John F. Kennedy Space Center near Cape Canaveral, the exciting city of Miami and the laid-back island of Key West. Many people from northern states, from nearby Cuba and other Caribbean nations and from South and Central America come to Florida to live permanently. As a result, Florida's population has doubled since 1980.

The increased population has created problems: Swamps have been drained to build houses, and new communities have increased pollution. Forests have been cut down to create farmland. Because of this building, many species of Florida's wildlife have become endangered. To fix this situation, Florida has tried to restore the Everglades. Located at Florida's southern tip, it is the largest subtropical wilderness in the U.S. and home to thousands of types of animals and plants.

THE FACT FILE

Area: 54,153 sq mi (140,256 sq km)

Population: 18,251,243

Capital: Tallahassee

Largest cities (with population):
Jacksonville (805,605)
Miami (409,719)
Tampa (336,823)

Entered Union (rank):
March 3, 1845 (27)

Motto: In God we trust

Tree: Sabal palm

Flower: orange blossom

Bird: mockingbird

Postal code: FL

DID YOU KNOW?

● In 1959, the U.S. experimented with sending mail by rocket. A guided missile carrying 3,000 letters was launched from Virginia and landed in Mayport, Florida, about 22 minutes later.

● Parts of Florida experience sinkholes—sudden openings in the ground. In 1999, a sinkhole opened under Lake Jackson, in Tallahassee, causing all of its water to disappear into the earth.

● The highest point in Florida is the lowest high point in any U.S. state.

The Everglades are wetlands that cover 5,000 sq mi (13,000 sq km).

ALABAMA

▲ Britton Hill

Pensacola

GEORGIA

⭐ **Tallahassee**

Apalachicola
National Forest

Jacksonville
Mayport

Saint Augustine

Ocala
National
Forest

Ocala
Silver
Springs

St. Johns River

Orlando

Walt Disney World

Cape Canaveral/
John F. Kennedy
Space Center

Tampa
Saint Petersburg

Gulf of Mexico

Sarasota

Kissimmee R.

Lake
Okeechobee

Atlantic Ocean

N
W ⬥TFK⬥ E
S

The Everglades

Fort Lauderdale

Miami Beach
Miami
Homestead

Everglades National Park

Florida Keys

Key West

0   50   100 mi
0   50   100   150 km

TFK TOP 5

1 Highest point: Britton Hill,
345 feet (105 m)

2 Longest river: St. Johns River,
275 miles (443 km)

3 Largest lake: Lake Okeechobee,
730 sq mi (1,890 sq km)

4 Biggest spring: Silver Springs,
near Ocala, producing 500 million
gallons (1,893 million L) of water a day

5 Oldest European city:
St. Augustine, founded 1565

Discovery is one of the
space shuttles launched
from the Kennedy Space
Center.

ROADSIDE FUN

**Edward Leedskalnin
spent 28 years building
the Coral Castle in
Homestead** to impress
an ex-girlfriend. Inside and
out, the castle is made of
more than 2 million pounds
(907,184 kg) of stone
blocks—from the furniture
to a fountain to a nine-ton
gate. The stone blocks
weigh as much as 30 tons
each, yet Leedskalnin built
everything himself by hand.

Florida

Georgia

The skyline of Atlanta

The city of Savannah represents the Old South. Founded in 1733, it is full of beautiful old preserved houses and squares. The past is important in **GEORGIA**, but so is the future. Atlanta, known as the capital of the New South, is a communications and transportation center. It is the headquarters of many large companies, and its airport is the busiest in the U.S. Georgia once enforced strict segregation laws, but today Georgia is more and more an integrated society. African Americans make up about 30 percent of the state's population, and Atlanta has the sixth largest black population of any U.S. city. Not only is Georgia the biggest state east of the Mississippi, but it has one of the fastest-growing populations, with a large number of immigrants.

Agriculture is big in Georgia's economy: the state leads the nation in peanut production. Pecans, corn and peaches are among crops that are grown in the farmlands in the central part of the state, between the Appalachian Mountains in the north and the low-lying Coastal Plain in the south. But manufacturing, especially of textiles, paper products and transportation equipment, has become the most important part of the economy. Still, despite its new attitude and economy, Georgia keeps its Southern charm and physical beauty. You can find them in such places as the Blue Ridge Mountain area, the Okefenokee National Wildlife Refuge and the Cumberland Island National Seashore.

THE FACT FILE

Area: 57,919 sq mi (150,010 sq km)

Population: 9,544,750

Capital: Atlanta

Largest cities (with population):
Atlanta (519,145)
Augusta (192,142)
Columbus (185,781)

Entered Union (rank):
January 2, 1788 (4)

Motto: Wisdom, justice and moderation

Tree: live oak

Flower: Cherokee rose

Bird: brown thrasher

Postal code: GA

DID YOU KNOW?

● The Confederate Memorial Carving, located in Stone Mountain Park, shows Confederate president Jefferson Davis and generals Robert E. Lee and "Stonewall" Jackson on horseback. The statue, carved into the side of a mountain, is 90 feet (27 m) high and 190 feet (57 m) wide.

● Coca-Cola was invented by druggist John S. Pemberton in Columbus in 1885.

● Berry College, in Rome, has the largest campus in the U.S. At about 40 sq mi (103 sq km), it is nearly twice as big as Manhattan Island, New York.

The Stone Mountain Memorial Carving is bigger than a football field. Dynamite and jackhammers were used to "sculpt" the figures.

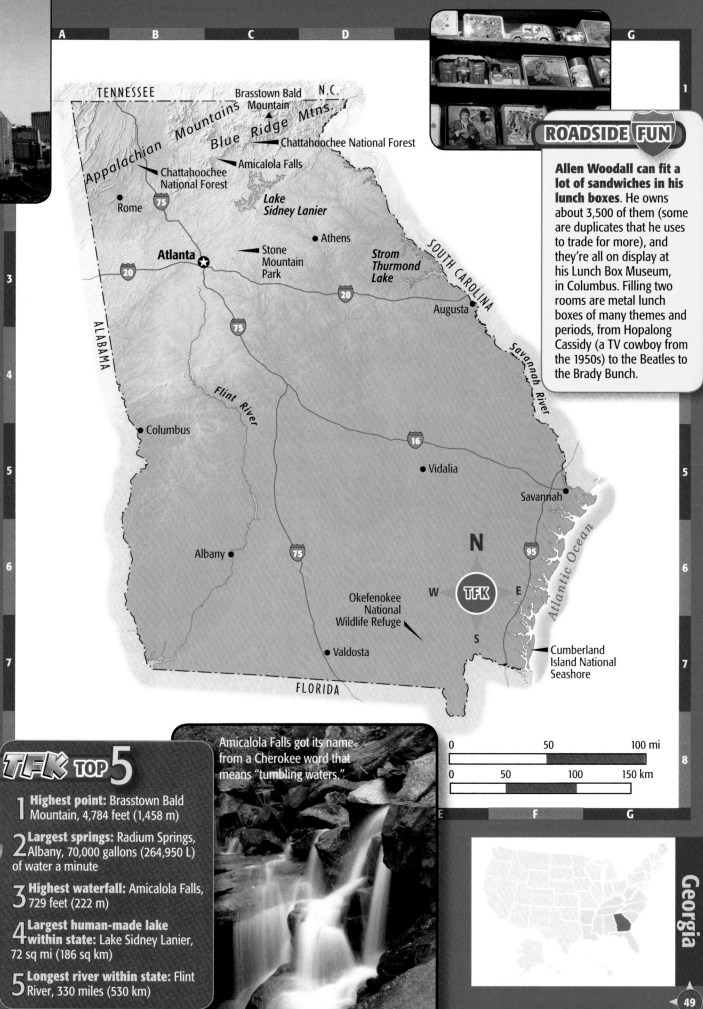

TENNESSEE

N.C.

Brasstown Bald
Mountain

Appalachian Mountains

Blue Ridge Mtns.

Chattahoochee National Forest

Chattahoochee
National Forest

Amicalola Falls

*Lake
Sidney Lanier*

Rome

Athens

Atlanta

Stone
Mountain
Park

*Strom
Thurmond
Lake*

SOUTH CAROLINA

Augusta

ALABAMA

Savannah River

Flint River

Columbus

Vidalia

Savannah

N

Atlantic Ocean

W TFK E

Okefenokee
National
Wildlife Refuge

S

Albany

Valdosta

Cumberland
Island National
Seashore

FLORIDA

| 0 | 50 | 100 mi |
| 0 | 50 | 100 | 150 km |

ROADSIDE FUN

Allen Woodall can fit a lot of sandwiches in his lunch boxes. He owns about 3,500 of them (some are duplicates that he uses to trade for more), and they're all on display at his Lunch Box Museum, in Columbus. Filling two rooms are metal lunch boxes of many themes and periods, from Hopalong Cassidy (a TV cowboy from the 1950s) to the Beatles to the Brady Bunch.

Amicalola Falls got its name from a Cherokee word that means "tumbling waters."

TFK TOP 5

1 **Highest point:** Brasstown Bald Mountain, 4,784 feet (1,458 m)

2 **Largest springs:** Radium Springs, Albany, 70,000 gallons (264,950 L) of water a minute

3 **Highest waterfall:** Amicalola Falls, 729 feet (222 m)

4 **Largest human-made lake within state:** Lake Sidney Lanier, 72 sq mi (186 sq km)

5 **Longest river within state:** Flint River, 330 miles (530 km)

Georgia

Kentucky

In the 1800s, pioneers like Daniel Boone first passed through the Cumberland Gap and into a lush, green region that would become **KENTUCKY**—the first state west of the Allegheny Mountains. Many settlers continued west from Kentucky, but many also stayed. Kentucky still draws people for its beauty, especially its forested mountains in the east and the bluegrass of the central plains that feeds Thoroughbred horses. Kentucky's many human-made lakes and its 52 state parks draw hikers and boaters.

Kentucky has more miles of running water than any state except Alaska. These rivers and streams help irrigate Kentucky's 84,000 small farms that produce tobacco, soybeans and corn, as well as cattle and chickens. Close to half of the land in the state is forest, much of which is used commercially. Beneath southern Kentucky are spectacular cave systems. Coal is also underground— Kentucky is the third-largest coal producer in the U.S. Mining has spoiled the landscape in some places, but new regulations have been passed to prevent this from happening in the future.

THE FACT FILE

Area: 39,732 sq mi (102,907 sq km)

Population: 4,241,474

Capital: Frankfort

Largest cities (with population):
Lexington (279,044)
Louisville (245,315)
Owensboro (55,398)

Entered Union (rank):
June 1, 1792 (15)

Motto: United we stand, divided we fall

Tree: tulip poplar

Flower: goldenrod

Bird: Kentucky cardinal

Postal code: KY

DID YOU KNOW?

● Mammoth Caves in south-central Kentucky is the longest cave system in the world. About 360 miles (580 km) of it have been explored so far.

● The blades of Kentucky's bluegrass are green. But in spring and summer, the seed heads appear, and they are blue. If the grass isn't cut, fields of bluegrass are blue.

● About 60 percent of major leaguers use Louisville Slugger baseball bats. They are made in Louisville by the Hillerich & Bradsby company.

Except for the highway, the Cumberland Gap looks much as it did to early pioneers.

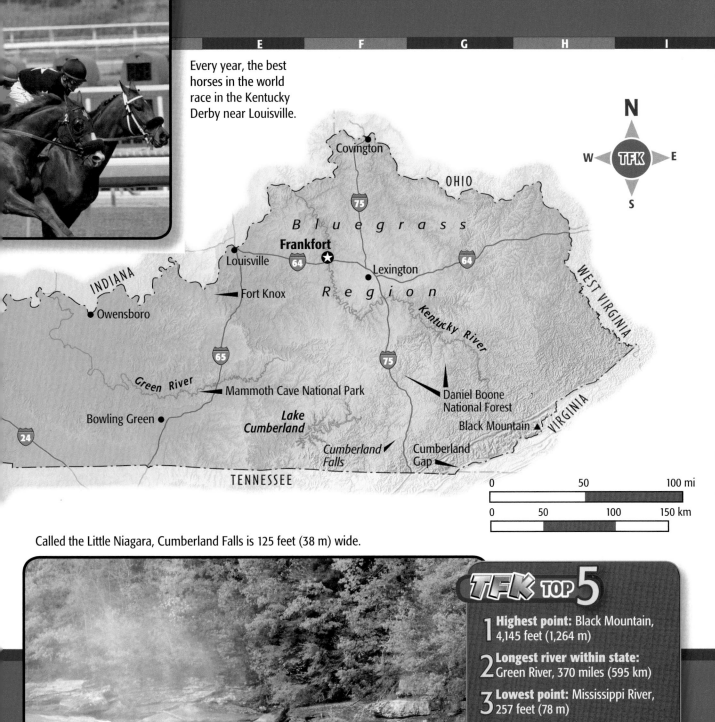

Every year, the best horses in the world race in the Kentucky Derby near Louisville.

Covington

OHIO

75

B l u e g r a s s

Frankfort **64**

Louisville

Lexington **64**

WEST VIRGINIA

INDIANA

Fort Knox

R e g i o n

Owensboro

Kentucky River

65

75

Green River

Mammoth Cave National Park

Daniel Boone National Forest

Bowling Green

Lake Cumberland

Black Mountain ▲

VIRGINIA

24

Cumberland Falls

Cumberland Gap

TENNESSEE

N

W   **TFK**   E

S

0   50   100 mi

0   50   100   150 km

Called the Little Niagara, Cumberland Falls is 125 feet (38 m) wide.

TFK TOP 5

1 Highest point: Black Mountain, 4,145 feet (1,264 m)

2 Longest river within state: Green River, 370 miles (595 km)

3 Lowest point: Mississippi River, 257 feet (78 m)

4 Largest human-made lake: Kentucky Lake, 260 sq mi (673 sq km)

5 Highest waterfall: Cumberland Falls, 68 feet (21 m)

Kentucky

Louisiana

Gumbo is a Louisiana stew that's often made with crawfish.

In August 2005, Hurricane Katrina struck the Gulf Coast, killing 1,577 Louisianans and causing $81 billion in damage. The storm shocked the nation because it destroyed much of New Orleans, America's most unique city. New Orleans is a special blend of cultures—Spanish, French, Caribbean, African American and Cajun (descendants of French-speaking people from Canada), with a few others thrown into the stew. New Orleans is where jazz began. **LOUISIANA** as a whole has its own food, music and easy-going way of life.

Louisiana's land, as well as its people, is one of a kind. The Mississippi River, which flows through the state and empties into the Gulf of Mexico, helps create vast areas of swamps, marshes and bayous that make up the state's wetlands. That equals about 40 percent of all the wetlands of the Lower 48 states. Rich soil is another gift from the Mississippi, and Louisiana farms grow crops including lots of sugarcane, cotton, rice and soybeans. In the northeast corner of the state, just west of the Mississippi, is a large region of grassy plains and hills, as well as forests that are cut for timber. Louisiana is also one of the top oil- and natural-gas-producing states. As Katrina's damage to New Orleans is repaired, tourism will once again bring much-needed income to the state's economy.

THE FACT FILE

Area: 43,566 sq mi (112,836 sq km)

Population: 4,293,204

Capital: Baton Rouge

Largest cities (with population):
New Orleans (239,124)
Baton Rouge (227,071)
Shreveport (199,569)

Entered Union (rank):
April 30, 1812 (18)

Motto: Union, justice and confidence

Tree: bald cypress

Flower: magnolia

Bird: eastern brown pelican

Postal code: LA

DID YOU KNOW?

● Every year, New Orleans holds Mardi Gras—a festival that takes place just before the Christian holiday of Ash Wednesday. Celebrators wear crazy costumes at parties and in parades.

● The biggest swamp in the U.S. is the Atchafalaya Swamp in south-central Louisiana. It is 930 sq mi (2,408 sq km).

● Baton Rouge's state capitol building is 450 feet (137 m) tall—the nation's highest state capitol.

The French Quarter is the oldest section of New Orleans.

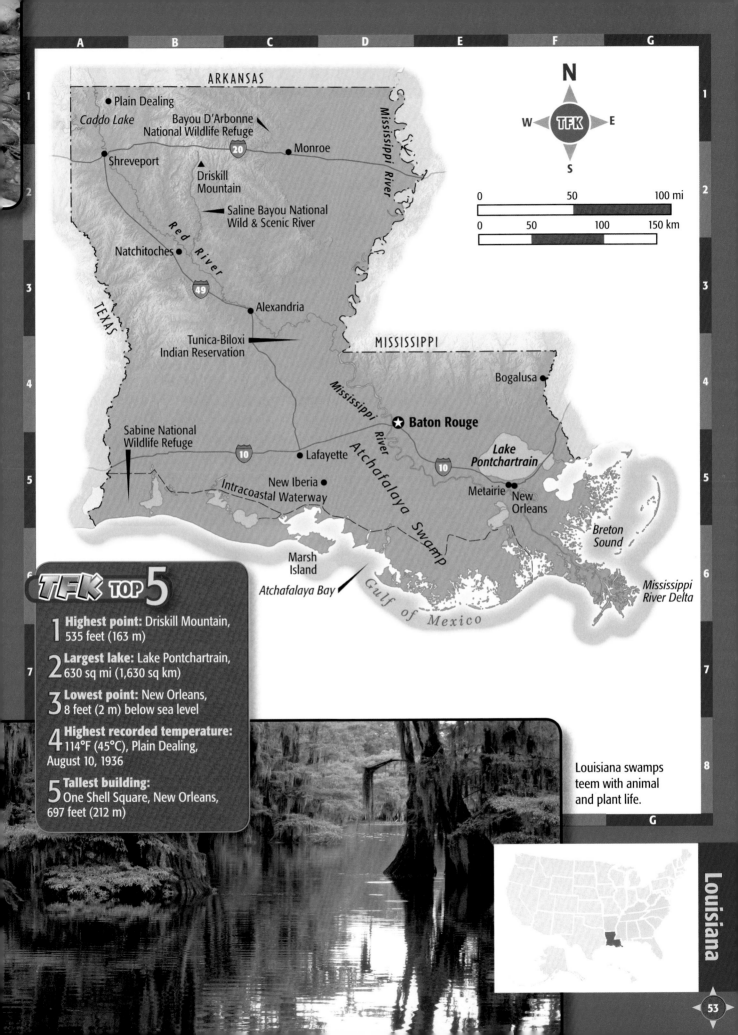

ARKANSAS

Plain Dealing

Caddo Lake

Bayou D'Arbonne National Wildlife Refuge

Monroe

20

Shreveport

Driskill Mountain

Saline Bayou National Wild & Scenic River

Natchitoches

Red River

49

TEXAS

Alexandria

Tunica-Biloxi Indian Reservation

MISSISSIPPI

Bogalusa

Mississippi River

Baton Rouge

Lake Pontchartrain

Sabine National Wildlife Refuge

10

Lafayette

Atchafalaya Swamp

10

Metairie

New Orleans

New Iberia

Intracoastal Waterway

Marsh Island

Atchafalaya Bay

Gulf of Mexico

Breton Sound

Mississippi River Delta

N
W — TFK — E
S

0	50	100 mi

0	50	100	150 km

TFK TOP 5

1 Highest point: Driskill Mountain, 535 feet (163 m)

2 Largest lake: Lake Pontchartrain, 630 sq mi (1,630 sq km)

3 Lowest point: New Orleans, 8 feet (2 m) below sea level

4 Highest recorded temperature: 114°F (45°C), Plain Dealing, August 10, 1936

5 Tallest building: One Shell Square, New Orleans, 697 feet (212 m)

Louisiana swamps teem with animal and plant life.

Louisiana

Mississippi

Dirty rice, a Mississippi treat, is often made with chicken livers.

MISSISSIPPI has changed slowly through the years. At one point, most people lived and worked in rural areas. Now, more and more people live in cities—small cities, to be sure. Mississippi has long been an agricultural state—its hills and prairies and delta area are rich farmland that once grew mostly cotton. Today, poultry has replaced cotton as the main agricultural moneymaker. And agriculture is no longer the largest part of Mississippi's economy. Most people work in service jobs, for military installations and in manufacturing. The state's Native Americans have also changed with the times: Thanks to their casinos, the Mississippi Band of Choctaw Indians is a major employer in eastern Mississippi.

One of the most famous Mississippi products is its music. This is the where the blues was born, the sad songs created by Robert Johnson, Howlin' Wolf and other black Delta musicians. And they had much to sing the blues about, as African Americans faced harsh discrimination in the state. In the 1960s, civil rights workers helped integrate Mississippi after violent opposition. Today, African Americans, who make up more than one-third of the state's population, are gaining more political and economic power.

THE FACT FILE

Area: 46,914 sq mi
(121,506 sq km)

Population: 2,918,785

Capital: Jackson

Largest cities (with population):
Jackson (175,710)
Gulfport (66,271)
Hattiesburg (50,233)

Entered Union (rank):
December 10, 1817 (20)

Motto: *Virtute et armis*
(By valor and arms)

Tree: magnolia

Flower: magnolia

Bird: mockingbird

Postal code: MS

DID YOU KNOW?

● The Mississippi Petrified Forest is filled with trees that have turned to stone over 35 million years.

● Dr. James D. Hardy performed the first heart transplant, an animal heart into a human, at the University of Mississippi Medical Center.

● Hush puppies, fried balls of dough, are a Mississippi treat. They supposedly got their name during the Civil War: Southern troops fed them to dogs so they wouldn't bark when Union troops were nearby.

Mississippi is famous for its Delta blues musicians.

The blossoms of the magnolia tree are very fragrant.

TENNESSEE

Southhaven

Holly Springs

Woodall Mountain ▲

Holly Springs National Forest

Oxford

Tupelo

Clarksdale

ARKANSAS

Mississippi River

Yazoo River

Mississippi Petrified Forest

Mississippi Choctow Reservation

Ross Barnett Reservoir

ALABAMA

Meridian

Vicksburg

★ Jackson

Natchez

Hattiesburg

DeSoto National Forest

N

LOUISIANA

W **TFK** E

S

0   50   100 mi

0   50   100   150 km

Gulfport   Biloxi

Gulf of Mexico

TFK TOP 5

1 Highest point: Woodall Mountain, 806 feet (246 m)

2 Lowest point: sea level, at the Gulf of Mexico

3 Highest recorded temperature: 115°F (46°C), Holly Springs, July 29, 1930

4 Largest national forest: De Soto National Forest, 591 sq mi (1,532 sq km)

5 Tallest building: Beau Rivage Casino Hotel, Biloxi, 347 feet (105 m)

In 2005, Hurricane Katrina damaged much of the Mississippi Gulf Coast.

Mississippi

North Carolina

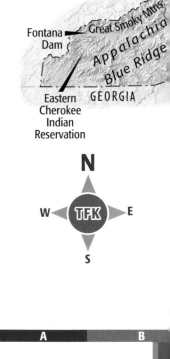

Cape Hatteras Lighthouse is the nation's tallest.

Fontana Dam
Great Smoky Mtns
Appalachia
Blue Ridge
Eastern Cherokee Indian Reservation
GEORGIA

N
W — TFK — E
S

NORTH CAROLINA begins not on the mainland but at the Outer Banks, a 175-mile (280 km) stretch of sandy barrier islands located off the Atlantic coast. They protect North Carolina from storms and attract beach and wildlife lovers. Across from the Outer Banks, Carolina's Coastal Plain extends about 100 miles (160 km) inland. Here are beaches, dunes, and swamps, including the Great Dismal Swamp.

Beyond the coast, in the central Piedmont region, the land gently rises. Most of the state's population lives here, and it is the location of historic old towns as well as big cities. The largest is Charlotte, which has become a major banking center. The Raleigh-Durham area is the site of many high-tech and medical-research centers. North Carolina is a major furniture manufacturer. Farmers in the Piedmont raise poultry and grow soybeans, sweet potatoes and other crops, including 40 percent of U.S. tobacco. West of the Piedmont are the Appalachian Mountains, which include the Blue Ridge and Great Smoky mountains. The state's rivers begin in the mountains and flow past pretty villages and spectacular scenery.

THE FACT FILE

Area: 48,718 sq mi (126,180 sq km)

Population: 9,061,032

Capital: Raleigh

Largest cities (with population):
Charlotte (671,588)
Raleigh (375,806)
Greensboro (247,183)

Entered Union (rank):
November 21, 1789 (12)

Motto: *Esse quam videri* (To be rather than to seem)

Tree: pine

Flower: dogwood

Bird: cardinal

Postal code: NC

DID YOU KNOW?

● Completed in 1895, the Biltmore House in Asheville is the largest privately owned home in the U.S. Constructed for the Vanderbilt family, the giant mansion has 250 rooms, 65 fireplaces and a bowling alley.

● The state of North Carolina began support of the University of North Carolina in 1795, making it the nation's oldest state university.

● The Croatan National Forest has the largest number of meat-eating plants of any national forest.

Charlotte has become a major financial center.

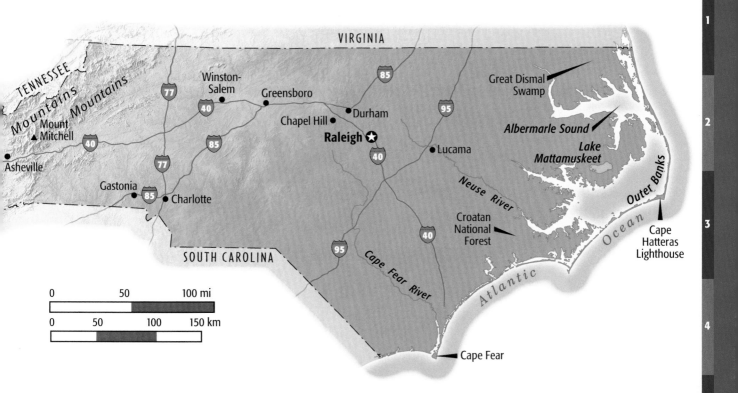

VIRGINIA

TENNESSEE

Mountains   Mountains

Mount
▲ Mitchell

Asheville

77   Winston-
Salem

40   Greensboro

Chapel Hill   Durham

Raleigh ★

85

95

Lucama

Great Dismal
Swamp

Albermarle Sound

*Lake
Mattamuskeet*

77

40   85

Gastonia   85   Charlotte

40

Neuse River

Croatan
National
Forest

Outer Banks

Atlantic

Ocean

Cape
Hatteras
Lighthouse

95   40

Cape Fear River

SOUTH CAROLINA

Cape Fear

0   50   100 mi

0   50   100   150 km

ROADSIDE FUN

Whirligigs are devices that spin in the wind, like weather vanes and windmills. Vollis Simpson's whirligigs are built from many different materials, including road signs, bicycle wheels and airplane parts. He paints them and sometimes covers them with small objects. About 30 are on display, some as tall as 50 feet (15 m), at Simpson's Windmill Park in Lucama. They don't power anything—except the imagination of those who see them.

TFK TOP 5

1 Highest point: Mount Mitchell, 6,684 feet (2,037 m)

2 Longest river within state: Neuse River, 248 miles (399 km)

3 Tallest dam: Fontana Dam, 480 feet (146 m)

4 Tallest brick lighthouse: Cape Hatteras Lighthouse, 215 feet (64 m)

5 Biggest natural lake: Lake Mattamuskeet, 15 miles (24 km) long, 6 miles (10 km) wide

Fontana Dam, the highest east of the Rockies, created a lake 30 miles (48 km) long.

North Carolina

South Carolina

Hilton Head Island is a popular vacation place.

Sassafras Mountain

Blue Ridge Mtns.

Sumter National Forest

Travel **SOUTH CAROLINA** from the west to the Atlantic coast and you will be heading downhill all the way—from up country to low country. The Blue Ridge Mountains rise up at the state's northwest tip. Rushing rivers lead southeast to the Piedmont Plateau, a region of gentle hills, where farmers grow peaches, soybeans and peanuts, and cotton that is used by large textile companies.

The region beyond the Piedmont is the Atlantic Coastal Plain, or low country. Approaching the coast, sandy hills and forests become wetlands. South Carolina has more swampland than any state except Louisiana. Vacation areas like Myrtle Beach dot the Atlantic shoreline. Just offshore are the Sea Islands, including the resorts of Hilton Head and Kiawah.

The most historic city in the Coastal Plain is Charleston. One of the busiest ports in the U.S., it offers a peek into South Carolina's past. Visitors can stroll past antebellum (pre-Civil War) houses, markets and churches and even a building where slaves were bought and sold.

THE FACT FILE

Area: 30,111 sq mi (77,988 sq km)

Population: 4,407,709

Capital: Columbia

Largest cities (with population):
Columbia (124,818)
Charleston (110,015)
North Charleston (91,421)

Entered Union (rank):
May 23, 1788 (8)

Motto: *Animis opibusque parati* (Prepared in mind and resources) and *Dum spiro spero* (While I breathe, I hope)

Tree: palmetto

Flower: yellow jessamine

Bird: Carolina wren

Postal code: SC

DID YOU KNOW?

● Parris Island, off South Carolina's coast, is a training base for the U.S. Marines.

● Many Hollywood movies have been filmed in the town of Beaufort, including *Forrest Gump*.

● The Gullah, who live in South Carolina's low country and some of the Sea Islands, are descendants of enslaved Africans and have held onto much of their West African culture.

Beautiful Beaufort was founded in 1711.

A few peaks in South Carolina's Blue Ridge Mountains are higher than 3,000 feet (914 m).

0   50   100 mi

0   50   100   150 km

N
W ← TFK → E
S

Spartanburg
Rock Hill

NORTH CAROLINA

Sumter
National
Forest

Camden ●   20

★ **Columbia**

95

95

*Lake
Marion*

Myrtle Beach ●

Santee River

Ocean

Francis Marion
National Forest

GEORGIA

Savannah River

26

20

26

95

North Charleston
Charleston ● ● Mt. Pleasant

Kiawah Island

Beaufort ●

Atlantic

Parris Island

Hilton Head Island

Charleston has many
historic houses.

TFK TOP 5

1 **Highest point:** Sassafras
Mountain, 3,560 feet (1,085 m)

2 **Longest river within state:**
The Savannah River, 314 miles
(505 km)

3 **Tallest building:** Capitol Center,
Columbia, 349 feet (106 m)

4 **Highest recorded temperature:**
111°F (43°C), Camden,
June 28, 1954

5 **Largest human-made lake:**
Lake Marion, 172 sq mi (445 sq km)

Tennessee

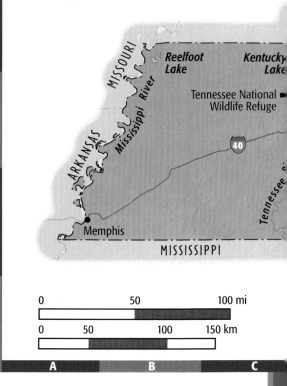

Two major geographical features form the east and west boundaries of **TENNESSEE**. The Appalachian mountain chain creates the eastern border. The Great Smoky Mountains, a part of the Appalachians, have six peaks higher than 5,000 feet (1,524 m). East Tennessee is a rugged area that has been mined for coal and other minerals.

The western border of Tennessee is formed by the Mississippi River. West Tennessee is a hilly, fertile area called the Gulf Coastal Plain where farmers grow cotton and soybeans. Between East and West Tennessee is, naturally enough, Middle Tennessee, a fertile area with plenty of grazing land for cattle.

Two great musical traditions in Tennessee are blues and country. The city of Memphis has been a magnet for blues musicians for many years. The blues is a type of music that was created by African Americans in the South. Great blues musicians, including John Lee Hooker and B.B. King, came from all over—and still come—to Beale Street in Memphis to write and perform. Tennessee is also famous for country music. Nashville, known as the capital of country music, is the location of the Grand Ole Opry, a theater whose acts, from Hank Williams to Carrie Underwood, have been broadcast over the radio since 1925.

THE FACT FILE

Area: 41,220 sq mi (106,759 sq km)

Population: 6,156,719

Capital: Nashville

Largest cities (with population):
Memphis (674,028)
Nashville (590,807)
Knoxville (183,546)

Entered Union (rank):
June 1, 1796 (16)

Motto: Agriculture and commerce

Tree: tulip poplar

Flower: iris

Bird: mockingbird

Postal code: TN

DID YOU KNOW?

● Tennessee is one of only two states (Missouri is the other) that border on eight states.

● Graceland, in Memphis, is the mansion that belonged to Elvis Presley. It is now a museum that displays just about everything owned by the King of Rock 'n' Roll.

● Knoxville was the site of the 1982 World's Fair. Just the symbol of the Fair remains—the Sunsphere, a 266-foot (81 m) steel tower topped by a 75-foot (23 m) globe.

The Great Smoky Mountains got their name from fog that sometimes hangs above the forests. From a distance, the fog looks like smoke.

D E F G H I J

1

KENTUCKY

Clarksville

24 65

Cumberland Mtns. VIRGINIA

Nashville

40 Norris Lake

75 Cherokee
National
Forest

Oak Ridge

Murfreesboro 40 Mountains

Duck River Knoxville NORTH CAROLINA

2

Tennessee River Gatlinburg

yville

65 24 75 Appalachian Clingmans
Dome

Great Smoky Mtns.

Chattanooga Cherokee
National Forest

3

ALABAMA GEORGIA

N

W **TFK** E

S

TFK TOP 5

1 **Highest point:** Clingmans Dome,
6,643 feet (2,026 m)

2 **Longest river within state:** Duck
River, 269 miles (432 km)

3 **Biggest human-made lake:** Kentucky Lake, 250 sq mi (649 sq km)

4 **Highest recorded temperature:**
113°F (45°C), Perryville, August 9,
1930

5 **Tallest building:** AT&T Building,
Nashville, 617 feet (188 m)

The AT&T Building (far left) stands out in
the Nashville skyline.

Country music's greatest
acts play at the Grand
Ole Opry.

GRAND OLE OPRY

650 WSM GRAND OLE OPRY www.OPRY.com

61

Virginia

The U.S. government plays a large role in Virginians' lives. With the Pentagon, the CIA and the Norfolk Naval Base all located in Virginia, the Federal Government is the Old Dominion's biggest employer. Many people who work for the government in Washington, D.C., live in Virginia. Of course, Virginia has attracted other big businesses, including the publishing company Gannett and the candy company Mars, as well as many high-tech companies. Farming, too, is important to Virginia's economy. The state's many small farms produce tomatoes, soybeans, tobacco and other crops.

Eastern Virginia, known as the Tidewater, is a series of large peninsulas surrounding Chesapeake Bay. Along the Atlantic coast are ports for shipping and beaches for vacationing. Much of the Tidewater is low and marshy, but moving west the land slowly rises to the gentle hills of the Piedmont region. Farther west are the Blue Ridge Mountains and beyond them the Allegheny Mountains. Between these ranges are fertile valleys, including the Shenandoah Valley. Early settlers in wagons traveled south through it to seek a new home. Today, tourists drive through it to admire the scenery.

THE FACT FILE

Area: 39,598 sq mi (102,558 sq km)

Population: 7,712,091

Capital: Richmond

Largest cities (with population):
Virginia Beach (434,743)
Norfolk (235,747)
Chesapeake (219,154)

Entered Union (rank):
June 25, 1788 (10)

Motto: *Sic semper tyrannis* (Thus always to tyrants)

Tree: dogwood

Flower: dogwood

Bird: cardinal

Postal code: VA

DID YOU KNOW?

● Eight U.S. Presidents were born in Virginia: George Washington, Thomas Jefferson, James Madison, James Monroe, William Henry Harrison, John Tyler, Zachary Taylor and Woodrow Wilson.

● Naval Station Norfolk in Hampton Roads, home of the U.S. Navy's Atlantic fleet, is the largest naval base in the world.

● The 20-mile (32 km) Chesapeake Bay Bridge-Tunnel connects the Delmarva Peninsula to the rest of Virginia.

TFK TOP 5

1 Highest point: Mount Rogers, 5,729 feet (1,746 m)

2 Longest river within the state: James River, 410 miles (660 km)

3 Lowest point: sea level at the Atlantic Ocean

4 Largest building: the Pentagon, Arlington County, 29 acres (11 ha), plus 5 acres (2 ha) of central courtyard

5 Largest body of water: Buggs Island Lake (John H. Kerr Reservoir), 76 sq mi (198 sq km)

KENTUCKY
Allegheny
Mount Rog
TENNESSEE

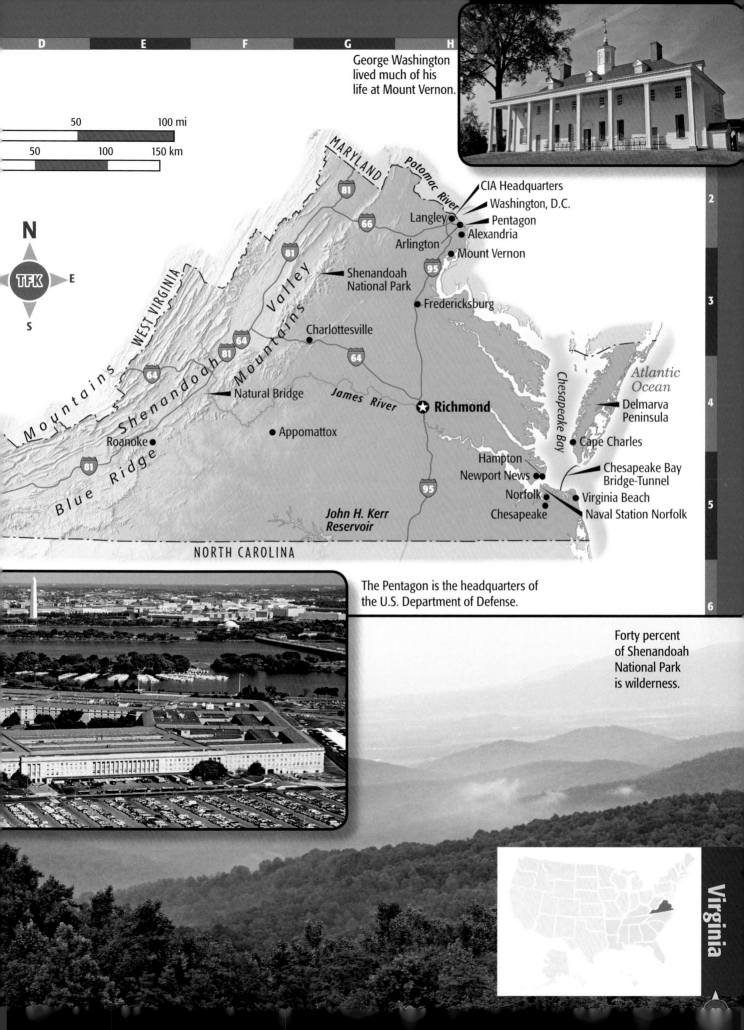

George Washington lived much of his life at Mount Vernon.

50   **100 mi**

50   **100**   **150 km**

N
TFK
E
S

MARYLAND

Potomac River

81

66

81

CIA Headquarters
Washington, D.C.
Langley
Pentagon
Alexandria
Arlington
Mount Vernon

95

Shenandoah National Park

WEST VIRGINIA

2

3

Fredericksburg

64

81

Charlottesville

64

Atlantic Ocean

Mountains

Valley

Shenandoah

Mountains

4

Natural Bridge

James River

Richmond

Delmarva Peninsula

Chesapeake Bay

64

Appomattox

Cape Charles

Roanoke

Blue Ridge

81

Hampton
Newport News

Chesapeake Bay Bridge-Tunnel

95

Norfolk

Virginia Beach

Chesapeake

Naval Station Norfolk

John H. Kerr Reservoir

5

NORTH CAROLINA

6

The Pentagon is the headquarters of the U.S. Department of Defense.

Forty percent of Shenandoah National Park is wilderness.

Virginia

West Virginia

WEST VIRGINIA got its nickname for good reason: the entire state is part of the Appalachian Mountain system. The average elevation of West Virginia—1,500 feet (458 m)—is the highest of any state east of the Mississippi River. The land is so rugged that it has very few farms. But under the land is a natural resource worth harvesting—coal. Only Wyoming produces more coal than West Virginia. About 70 percent of the state is covered by forest, which is why the timber industry is important to West Virginia. But more than 1,562 sq mi (4,045 sq km) have been set aside for public use in 48 state parks and recreation areas, nine state forests and two national forests, including the Monongahela National Forest.

Coal is an important resource in West Virginia.

The biggest source of income to West Virginia is tourism, which is one of the reasons lawmakers have tried to protect the state's natural beauty from coal mining. Whitewater rafters enjoy West Virginia's rivers, and skiers enjoy its wintry slopes. Mountains also come in handy for rock climbers, and hikers and bikers make use of trails like the Appalachian National Scenic Trail and North Bend Trail.

THE FACT FILE

Area: 24,087 sq mi (62,384 sq km)

Population: 1,812,035

Capital: Charleston

Largest cities (with population):
Charleston (50,478)
Huntington (48,982)
Parkersburg (31,617)

Entered Union (rank):
June 20, 1863 (35)

Motto: *Montani semper liberi*
(Mountaineers are always free)

Tree: sugar maple

Flower: rhododendron

Bird: cardinal

Postal code: WV

DID YOU KNOW?

● When Virginia broke away from the Union at the start of the Civil War, the western part of the state did not. President Abraham Lincoln granted this region, West Virginia, statehood in 1863.

● The worst mining disaster in U.S. history took place on December 6, 1907, when an explosion in a West Virginia coal mine killed 362 workers.

● In 1921, West Virginia became the first state to have a sales tax.

The Monongahela National Forest has 700 miles (1,126 km) of hiking trails.

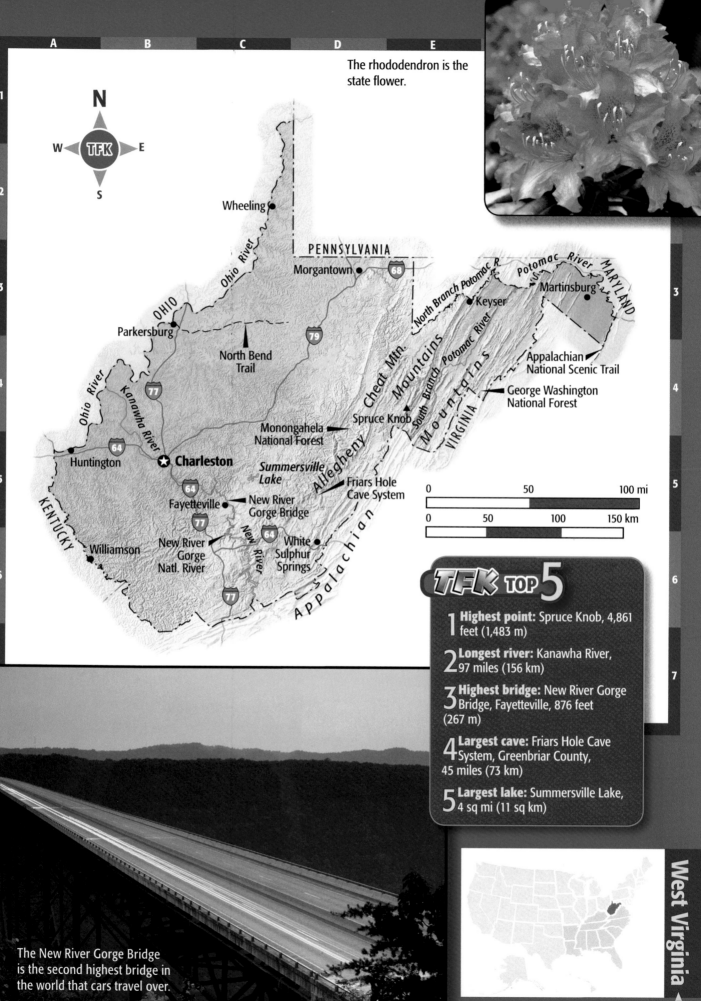

A B C D E

N
W ⟨TFK⟩ E
S

The rhododendron is the state flower.

1

2

Wheeling

PENNSYLVANIA

Morgantown ● 68

OHIO

Ohio River

Parkersburg ●

North Bend Trail

79

North Branch Potomac R.

Potomac River

MARYLAND

Martinsburg ●

Keyser ●

Cheat Mtn.

Mountains

South Branch Potomac River

Appalachian National Scenic Trail

3

Ohio River

77

Kanawha River

Spruce Knob

Monongahela National Forest

Allegheny

Mountains

VIRGINIA

George Washington National Forest

4

64

Huntington ●

★ Charleston

Summersville Lake

64

Fayetteville ●

New River Gorge Bridge

Friars Hole Cave System

0   50   100 mi
0   50   100   150 km

5

KENTUCKY

77

New River Gorge Natl. River

New River

64

White Sulphur Springs

6

Williamson ●

77

Appalachian

TFK TOP 5

1 **Highest point:** Spruce Knob, 4,861 feet (1,483 m)

2 **Longest river:** Kanawha River, 97 miles (156 km)

3 **Highest bridge:** New River Gorge Bridge, Fayetteville, 876 feet (267 m)

4 **Largest cave:** Friars Hole Cave System, Greenbriar County, 45 miles (73 km)

5 **Largest lake:** Summersville Lake, 4 sq mi (11 sq km)

The New River Gorge Bridge is the second highest bridge in the world that cars travel over.

Midwest

During several Ice Ages that took place over millions of years, glaciers covered the Midwest region. They not only flattened much of the land but left behind rich soil. That soil now produces much of the nation's supply of wheat, corn, soybeans and other crops. In the 1800s, immigrants came by the thousands to farm the land and to dig for minerals. Many arrived from northern Europe, and their descendants continue to farm the fertile soil of the Midwest. In the 21st century, manufacturing is as important as agriculture had been to the region's economy. The Midwest's central location—as well as its rivers, railroad lines, interstate highways and access to the Great Lakes—makes it easy for businesses to send products across the country and to other nations.

The region has abundant farmland, but it also has some great cities, such as Chicago, St. Louis and Indianapolis. And not all the land is flat prairie. There are awesome landscapes, from the Badlands of Nebraska to the forests of Wisconsin to the sand dunes of Lake Michigan.

The North Breakwater Light in Ludington, Michigan, rises 57 feet (17 m) over Lake Michigan.

Chicago is the largest city in the Midwest and the third largest in the U.S.

THE FACT FILE

States: Illinois, Indiana, Iowa, Kansas, Michigan, Minnesota, Missouri, Nebraska, North Dakota, Ohio, South Dakota, Wisconsin
Area: 773,241 sq mi (2,002,685 sq km)
Population: 66,388,795
Highest point: Harney Peak, South Dakota, 7,242 feet (2,208 m)
Lowest point: St. Francis River, Missouri, 230 feet (70 m)
Largest state: Minnesota, 84,402 sq mi (218,601 sq km)
Smallest state: Indiana, 35,870 sq mi (92,904 sq km)
Most populous state: Illinois, 12,852,548
Least populous state: North Dakota, 639,715

DID YOU KNOW?

● The Great Flood of 1993 covered parts of all Midwestern states except Indiana, Michigan and Ohio, killing 50 people and leaving tens of thousands of people homeless.

● Young Abraham Lincoln lived on an Indiana farm in what is now Lincoln City from 1816 to 1830, when he left for Illinois. Indiana's Lincoln Boyhood National Memorial and the Abraham Lincoln Presidential Library and Museum in Springfield, Illinois, detail his life.

● Fifty percent of the population of the U.S. lives within 500 miles of Ohio.

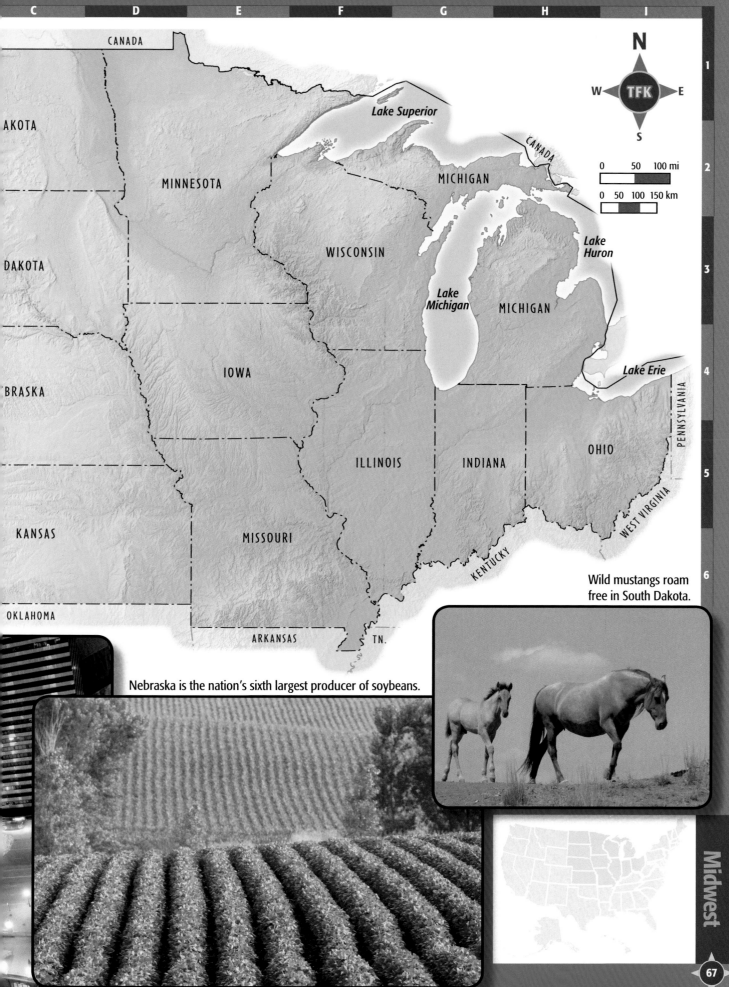

CANADA

N

W ⬥TFK⬥ E

S

Lake Superior

CANADA

0   50   100 mi

0   50 100 150 km

AKOTA

MINNESOTA

MICHIGAN

DAKOTA

WISCONSIN

Lake
Huron

Lake
Michigan

MICHIGAN

BRASKA

IOWA

Lake Erie

PENNSYLVANIA

KANSAS

ILLINOIS

INDIANA

OHIO

MISSOURI

WEST VIRGINIA

KENTUCKY

OKLAHOMA

ARKANSAS   TN.

Wild mustangs roam
free in South Dakota.

Nebraska is the nation's sixth largest producer of soybeans.

Midwest

Illinois

Chicago's popular Millennium Park displays the works of famous artists and architects. The Cloud Gate, nicknamed "the Bean," is the park's most well-known sculpture.

ILLINOIS

ILLINOIS is a hub of the nation. The state's transportation system and location in the middle of the country allow it easy access to markets in the rest of the country. That's why many industries began here, especially in and around Chicago, the third largest city in the U.S. It has been the center of meatpacking and steelmaking. With its promise of jobs, Chicago was a magnet for European immigrants as well as for African Americans from the South. Today about half of the state's population lives in the greater Chicago metropolitan area.

Outside of Chicago, most of Illinois was once prairie, except for the hilly northwest and a small area in the south called the Shawnee Hills. Now farms cover 65 percent of the rich land. Farmers raise hogs and grow the second-biggest crops of corn and soybeans in the nation, mostly in the large Central Plains region. The southern tip of the state, where the Mississippi and Ohio rivers meet, is part of the Gulf Coastal Plain. Cotton is grown in this swampy, wet region. Illinois is the fourth largest industrial state. It manufactures farm equipment, food products, drugs and medicines, and metal products.

THE FACT FILE

Area: 57,915 sq mi (149,999 sq km)
Population: 12,852,548
Capital: Springfield
Largest cities (with population):
Chicago (2,836,658)
Aurora (170,855)
Rockford (156,596)
Entered Union (rank):
December 3, 1818 (21)
Motto: State sovereignty, national union
Tree: white oak
Flower: violet
Bird: cardinal
Postal code: IL

DID YOU KNOW?

● The World's Columbian Exposition of 1893 was held in Chicago and introduced these for the first time: the Ferris wheel, picture postcards, Shredded Wheat, Cracker Jack and Cream of Wheat.

● The Abraham Lincoln Presidential Library and Museum in Springfield has a copy of the Gettysburg Address handwritten by Lincoln.

● Illinois is the nation's leading grower of pumpkins. In 2007, it produced 542 million pounds (nearly 246 million kg) of

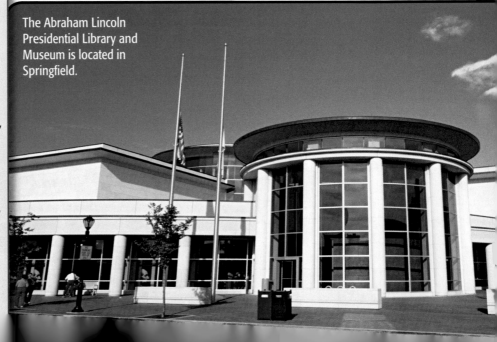

The Abraham Lincoln Presidential Library and Museum is located in Springfield.

WISCONSIN

▲ Charles Mound

● Rockford

Waukegan ●

Lake Michigan

Evanston ●

Naperville ●

Aurora ●

● Chicago

IOWA

● Moline

● Joliet

Mississippi River

Illinois River

55

57

74

● Peoria

74

74

● Urbana

INDIANA

72

Springfield ⭐

Lincoln Home National Historical Site

72

57

MISSOURI

55

70

70

70

55

Carlyle Lake

N

W TFK E

S

Mississippi River

57

Shawnee National Forest

● Carbondale

Ohio River

● Metropolis

KENTUCKY

0   50   100 mi
0   50   100   150 km

The Willis Tower (formerly called the Sears Tower) in Chicago has been the tallest building in the U.S. since 1973.

HAM LINCOLN PRESIDENT

TFK TOP 5

1 Highest point: Charles Mound, 1,235 feet (376 m)

2 Longest river within state: Illinois River, 273 miles (439 km)

3 Lowest point: 279 feet (85 m) at the Mississippi River

4 Biggest human-made lake: Carlyle Lake, 38 sq mi (98 sq km)

5 Tallest building: Willis Tower, Chicago, 1,450 feet (442 m)

Illinois

Indiana

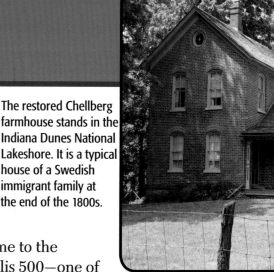

The restored Chellberg farmhouse stands in the Indiana Dunes National Lakeshore. It is a typical house of a Swedish immigrant family at the end of the 1800s.

Every year on Memorial Day, about 400,000 people come to the Indianapolis Motor Speedway to watch the Indianapolis 500—one of the greatest car races in the world. Cars are important to Indiana in other ways. Thirteen interstate highways pass through it—the most of any state. And the production of cars and car parts is a big part of Indiana's economy. Concentrated in the Calumet Region, in the northwest, industrial cities such as Gary and Hammond make cars, as well as steel, aircraft parts, farm machinery and medical drugs.

Not all of the region is industrial, however. The shores of Lake Michigan have beautiful sand dunes, and farther south is a landscape of lakes and farmland. Toward the east is green countryside dotted with peaceful Amish communities. Central Indiana is a gently rolling region where farms take advantage of the fertile soil. The major crops grown here are corn, including the corn used to make popcorn, and soybeans. Indiana farmers raise everything from ducks to ostriches and llamas. The southern part of the state has forests, valleys and gorges. Large amounts of coal are mined here, while in south-central Indiana, quarry workers dig limestone used to make buildings and roads. This region is known for its many caves, including Wyandotte Cave, one of the largest in the U.S.

THE FACT FILE

Area: 35,870 sq mi (92,904 sq km)
Population: 6,345,289
Capital: Indianapolis
Largest cities (with population):
Indianapolis (795,458)
Fort Wayne (251,247)
Evansville (116,253)
Entered Union (rank):
December 11, 1816 (19)
Motto: The crossroads of America
Tree: tulip tree
Flower: peony
Bird: cardinal
Postal code: IN

DID YOU KNOW?

● On the evening of March 31, 1880, Wabash became the world's first city to be lit up by electric lights when a string of lights atop the city's courthouse was turned on.

● Chrysler High School's fieldhouse in New Castle seats 9,314 people, making it the largest high school gym in the country. Of the 10 largest high school gyms by seating capacity in the U.S., Indiana has nine.

● The post office in Santa Claus, Indiana, gets very busy around Christmas. It receives letters addressed to Santa Claus from all around the world.

The Indianapolis 500 is the biggest and oldest motor race held in the U.S.

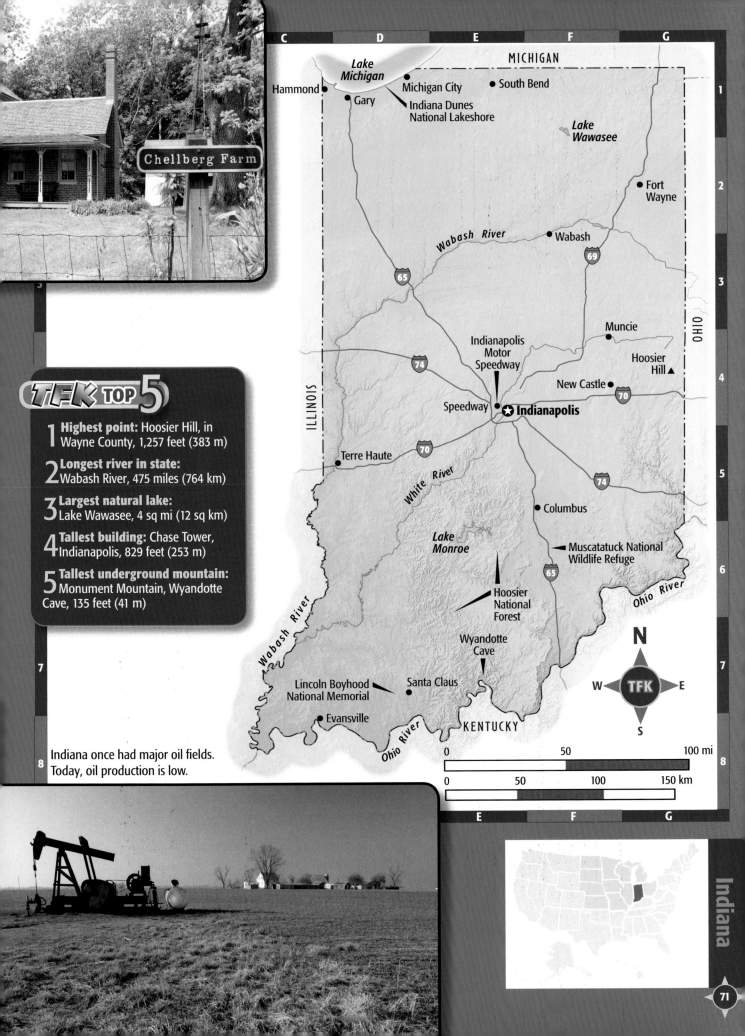

Chellberg Farm

MICHIGAN

Lake Michigan

Hammond
Gary
Michigan City
South Bend
Indiana Dunes National Lakeshore

Lake Wawasee

Fort Wayne

Wabash River
Wabash

65

69

Muncie

Hoosier Hill ▲

Indianapolis Motor Speedway

74

New Castle

70

Speedway
★ Indianapolis

ILLINOIS

OHIO

Terre Haute

70

White River

74

Columbus

Lake Monroe

Muscatatuck National Wildlife Refuge

65

Ohio River

Hoosier National Forest

Wyandotte Cave

Wabash River

N

W TFK E

S

Lincoln Boyhood National Memorial
Santa Claus

Evansville

Ohio River

KENTUCKY

0   50   100 mi

0   50   100   150 km

TFK TOP 5

1 **Highest point:** Hoosier Hill, in Wayne County, 1,257 feet (383 m)

2 **Longest river in state:** Wabash River, 475 miles (764 km)

3 **Largest natural lake:** Lake Wawasee, 4 sq mi (12 sq km)

4 **Tallest building:** Chase Tower, Indianapolis, 829 feet (253 m)

5 **Tallest underground mountain:** Monument Mountain, Wyandotte Cave, 135 feet (41 m)

Indiana once had major oil fields. Today, oil production is low.

Indiana

Iowa

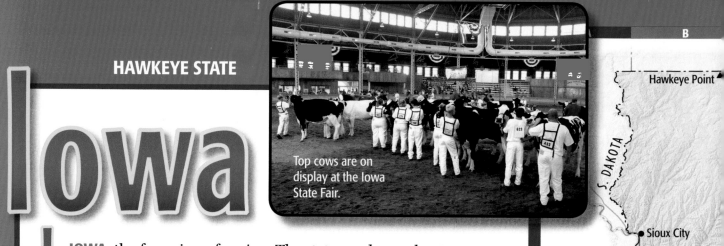

Top cows are on display at the Iowa State Fair.

Hawkeye Point

S. DAKOTA

NEBRASKA

Sioux City

Missouri River

Council Bluffs

In **IOWA**, the focus is on farming. The state produces about 10 percent of the food supply of the U.S. After California and Texas, Iowa is the third most productive agricultural state. It is the nation's No. 1 producer of corn and soybeans and raises more hogs than any other state. Much of the state's manufacturing is food related, from cattle processing to producing breakfast cereal to building farm equipment. Iowa's soil is the reason for its agricultural success. Over the course of millions of years, advancing and retreating glaciers ground down the high points of the land and left behind drift, or layers of sand, clay and other materials—perfect soil for growing crops.

Those glaciers created three regions in what is now Iowa. In addition to drift, the flat Dissected Till Plains in southern and western Iowa were also covered by loess (say: *less*)—fertile soil carried by wind. The Young Drift Plains in north-central Iowa are even more fertile than the Till Plains. The northeast is called a Driftless Area. It has rugged hills and ridges, valleys and forests, and is a great place to explore nature for those who want a change from cornfields.

THE FACT FILE

Area: 55,875 sq mi (144,716 sq km)

Population: 2,988,046

Capital: Des Moines

Largest cities (with population):
Des Moines (196,998)
Cedar Rapids (126,396)
Davenport (98,975)

Entered Union (rank):
December 28, 1846 (29)

Motto: Our liberties we prize and our rights we will maintain

Tree: oak

Flower: wild rose

Bird: eastern goldfinch

Postal code: IA

DID YOU KNOW?

● The U.S. government owns 0.1 percent of Iowa land—the lowest percentage of any state.

● The movie *Field of Dreams* was set and filmed in Iowa. It is about a man who builds a baseball diamond in his cornfield. The "field of dreams" constructed in Dyersville for the movie is a popular tourist attraction.

● The Amana Colonies in eastern Iowa is a religious community founded more than 150 years ago. In its seven villages, members all worked, ate and worshiped as a group. The villages are now a National Historic Landmark.

Big machines called combines harvest corn.

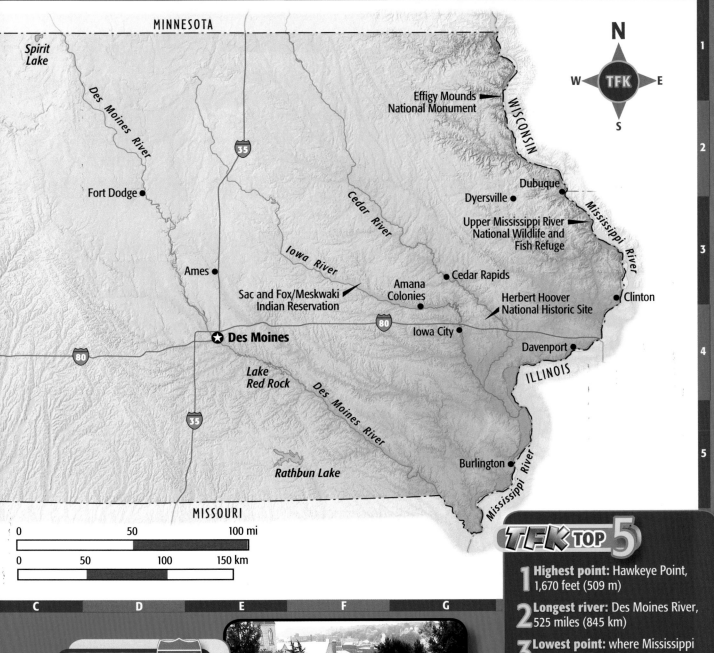

MINNESOTA

Spirit Lake

Des Moines River

Fort Dodge

35

WISCONSIN

Effigy Mounds National Monument

Dubuque

Dyersville

Upper Mississippi River National Wildlife and Fish Refuge

Cedar River

Mississippi River

Iowa River

Ames

Amana Colonies

Cedar Rapids

Clinton

Sac and Fox/Meskwaki Indian Reservation

Herbert Hoover National Historic Site

★ **Des Moines**

80

Iowa City

80

Davenport

ILLINOIS

Lake Red Rock

Des Moines River

Burlington

35

Mississippi River

Rathbun Lake

MISSOURI

N
W — TFK — E
S

0	50	100 mi

0	50	100	150 km

Iowa

TFK TOP 5

1 **Highest point:** Hawkeye Point, 1,670 feet (509 m)

2 **Longest river:** Des Moines River, 525 miles (845 km)

3 **Lowest point:** where Mississippi and Des Moines rivers meet, 480 feet (146 m)

4 **Largest natural lake:** Spirit Lake, 12 sq mi (30 sq km)

5 **Tallest building:** The Principal Building, Des Moines, 630 feet (192 m)

ROADSIDE FUN

Snake Alley, in Burlington, is known as the Crookedest Street in the World. Its builder wanted to connect two streets with a small street that looked like a winding vineyard path. The brick-laid alley has five half curves and two quarter curves in the space of 275 feet (83 m). It's not easy to drive in the best of conditions, which is why the lane is closed in winter.

Kansas

Kansas is the home of the Cessna Aircraft Company.

▲ Mount Sunflower

COLORADO

● Ulysses

Cimarron National Grassland

KANSAS has been called the breadbasket of the world. That's because the state usually leads the U.S. in wheat production (only North Dakota ever produces more). About 9 million acres are used to grow close to 300 million bushels yearly, which is enough wheat to make nearly 22 billion one-pound loaves of bread. Kansas farmers also grow corn and raise livestock. But it's manufacturing, not agriculture, that brings in the most money. In Kansas, building airplanes—including small private airplanes such as the Cessna and Learjet—is big business. Manufacturing food products, machinery and chemicals are economic strengths. So is the production of oil and natural gas.

Despite all its wheat fields, Kansas is not as flat as a table. In fact, the land rises steadily from east to west. Eastern Kansas, known as the Southeastern Plains, has forests, hills and valleys, as well as an area of grassy plains that support cattle ranches. Many of the state's larger cities are located in this region. West of the Central Lowlands, in the center of the state, are the vast prairies of the Great Plains. Wheat fields here and in the High Plains farther west stretch from horizon to horizon. Laura Ingalls Wilder wrote about her childhood on the Kansas plains in the classic novel *Little House on the Prairie*. Life in Kansas is different today, but much of the land itself remains the same.

KANSAS

THE FACT FILE

Area: 81,823 sq mi (211,922 sq km)

Population: 2,775,997

Capital: Topeka

Largest cities (with population):
Wichita (361,420)
Overland Park (169,403)
Kansas City (142,320)

Entered Union (rank):
January 29, 1861 (34)

Motto: *Ad astra per aspera*
(To the stars through difficulties)

Tree: cottonwood

Flower: sunflower

Bird: western meadowlark

Postal code: KS

DID YOU KNOW?

● Dodge City is the windiest city in the U.S. The average speed of winds there is nearly 14 mph (22 km/h).

● About two miles from Lebanon, a stone monument with a plaque marks the geographic center of the Lower 48 states, as established by the U.S. Geological Survey in 1941.

● Hutchinson sits on a vast underground field of salt, left from an ancient ocean. Factories have removed up to 5,000 barrels of salt a day for more than 20 years.

The state's wind turbines produce green energy.

NEBRASKA

N
W   TFK   E
S

1

Geographic center of → ● Lebanon
the 48 contiguous states

Kickapoo Indian Reservation ►

● Alton

Potawatomi Indian Reservation ►

Leavenworth ●

Smoky Hills

Milford Lake

70

Topeka ☆

Kansas City ●

2

Overland Park ●

70

Hays ●

Abilene ●

Lawrence ●

Olathe ●

Arkansas River

Tallgrass Prairie National Preserve ►

35

3

Missouri River

MISSOURI

135

Quivira National Wildlife Refuge

● Hutchinson

Fort Scott ●

4

Dodge City ●

Wichita ●

Flint Hills

Verdigris River

35

5

OKLAHOMA

0   50   100 mi

0   50   100   150 km

6

Grain elevators are known as Kansas skyscrapers.

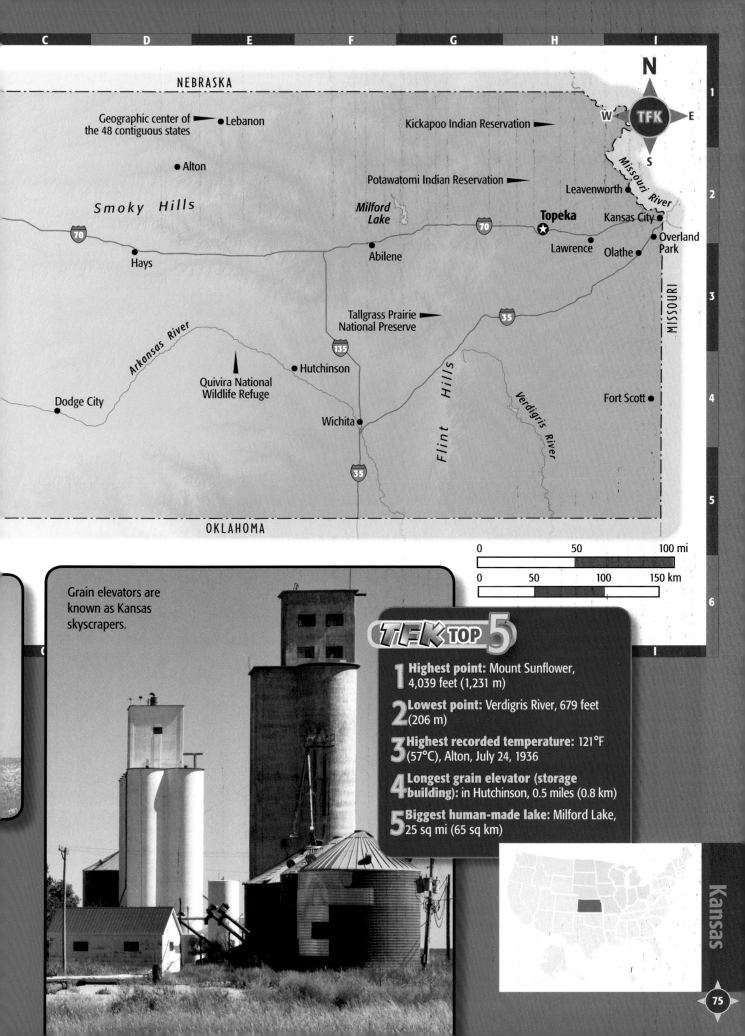

TFK TOP 5

1 Highest point: Mount Sunflower, 4,039 feet (1,231 m)

2 Lowest point: Verdigris River, 679 feet (206 m)

3 Highest recorded temperature: 121°F (57°C), Alton, July 24, 1936

4 Longest grain elevator (storage building): in Hutchinson, 0.5 miles (0.8 km)

5 Biggest human-made lake: Milford Lake, 25 sq mi (65 sq km)

Kansas

Michigan

Auto manufacturing has long been Michigan's most important industry.

Thanks to glaciers, **MICHIGAN** is surrounded on three sides by water. About 10,000 years ago, glaciers in North America cut grooves in the earth that filled with water. They became the four Great Lakes that border Michigan. The glaciers also formed the Straits of Mackinac, which now divide the state into two parts: the Upper (northern) and Lower (southern) peninsulas. The terrain of the Upper Peninsula varies from forests and hills filled with iron and copper to lowlands covered by swamps and farmland. The Lower Peninsula is a continuation of the lowlands. The region's moderate climate and rich soil make it ideal for growing fruits, vegetables and grains (cherries, celery and wheat, for example). There are also many dairy farms here.

Henry Ford had as big an effect on the state's economy as the glaciers did on its landscape. Thanks to Ford's car factories, the auto industry became vital to Michigan and the nation during the 20th century. Factories in Detroit, Dearborn, Flint and other Michigan cities are huge in the car business. Companies in the state manufacture chemicals, paper and breakfast cereal, among other products.

THE FACT FILE

Area: 58,527 sq mi (151,586 sq km)

Population: 10,071,822

Capital: Lansing

Largest cities (with population):
Detroit (916,952)
Grand Rapids (193,627)
Warren (134,223)

Entered Union (rank):
January 26, 1837 (26)

Motto: *Si quaeris peninsulam amoenam, circumspice* (If you seek a pleasant peninsula, look around you)

Tree: white pine

Flower: apple blossom

Bird: robin

Postal code: MI

DID YOU KNOW?

● The Mackinac Bridge is one of the longest suspension bridges in the world. Its main span is 8,344 feet (2,543 m) long.

● In 1894, Will Kellogg invented cornflakes while trying to make a vegetarian food for hospital patients. Today, Kellogg's, in Battle Creek, is a major producer of breakfast food.

● Residents of the Upper Peninsula call themselves Yoopers, pronouncing the region's initials (UP).

Mackinac Bridge connects the Upper and Lower peninsulas.

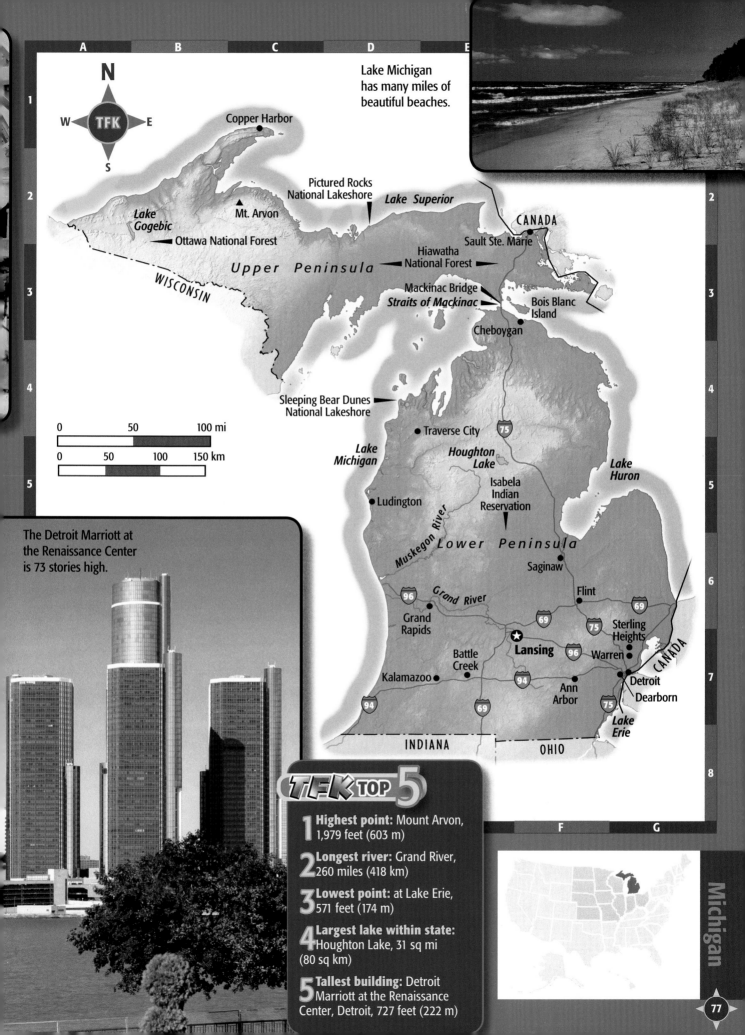

Lake Michigan has many miles of beautiful beaches.

Map Labels

Copper Harbor

Pictured Rocks National Lakeshore

Lake Superior

CANADA

Lake Gogebic

▲ Mt. Arvon

Ottawa National Forest

Sault Ste. Marie

Hiawatha National Forest

Upper Peninsula

WISCONSIN

Mackinac Bridge
Straits of Mackinac

Bois Blanc Island

Cheboygan

Sleeping Bear Dunes National Lakeshore

Traverse City

Lake Michigan

Houghton Lake

Lake Huron

Isabela Indian Reservation

Ludington

Muskegon River

Lower Peninsula

Saginaw

Grand River

Flint

Grand Rapids

Sterling Heights

★ **Lansing**

Warren

Battle Creek

Kalamazoo

Ann Arbor

Detroit
Dearborn

CANADA

Lake Erie

INDIANA

OHIO

Scale:
0 — 50 — 100 mi
0 — 50 — 100 — 150 km

The Detroit Marriott at the Renaissance Center is 73 stories high.

TFK TOP 5

1 Highest point: Mount Arvon, 1,979 feet (603 m)

2 Longest river: Grand River, 260 miles (418 km)

3 Lowest point: at Lake Erie, 571 feet (174 m)

4 Largest lake within state: Houghton Lake, 31 sq mi (80 sq km)

5 Tallest building: Detroit Marriott at the Renaissance Center, Detroit, 727 feet (222 m)

Michigan

Minnesota

MINNESOTA is the largest Midwestern state in land area, and it is the most northern state of the Lower 48. The winters are very cold—January temperatures in parts of the state average about -14°F (-25°C). But Minnesotans shrug off cold weather. They fish through holes in frozen lakes and rivers, cross-country ski, play ice hockey and snowmobile.

The weather doesn't hurt farmers. In the mostly level central and south regions, there are dairy farms and farms that grow sugar beets and corn. The northeast is called the Superior Upland, a region of low hills where iron ore has been mined, especially in the Mesabi range. One-third of the state is forested, and much of the timber is made into paper used by large publishing companies in Duluth and the Twin Cities of Minneapolis and St. Paul.

People enjoy the state's winter sports and events like the St. Paul Winter Carnival. They attend the world-famous Guthrie Theater in Minneapolis or hike through the Superior National Forest, one of the nation's largest. Or they may take the North Shore Scenic Drive along Lake Superior, past the farmlands, lakes and rivers that make Minnesota so beautiful.

ROADSIDE FUN

The Jolly Green Giant appeared in ads for the Green Giant food company and soon became a beloved character. In 1978, his statue was erected in Blue Earth, where the Green Giant Company once had a factory. The fiberglass statue is 55 feet (16 m) high.

THE FACT FILE

Area: 84,402 sq mi (218,601 sq km)

Population: 5,197,621

Capital: St. Paul

Largest cities (with population):
Minneapolis (377,392)
St. Paul (277,251)
Rochester (99,121)

Entered Union (rank):
May 11, 1858 (32)

Motto: *L'Étoile du nord* (Star of the North)

Tree: red (or Norway) pine

Flower: lady's slipper

Bird: common loon

Postal code: MN

DID YOU KNOW?

● "Land of 10,000 Lakes" is the state nickname that appears on Minnesota's license plates. But Minnesota really has about 12,000 lakes that are at least 10 acres (4 ha) in area, as well as many smaller ones.

● The Mall of America, in Bloomington, is one of the largest shopping malls in the world. It is 4.2 million sq ft (390,000 sq m), big enough to contain seven Yankee Stadiums.

● The mighty Mississippi River begins in northwest Minnesota at Lake Itasca, which is less than 2 sq mi (3 sq km) in area.

Minneapolis and the nearby city of St. Paul are known as the Twin Cities.

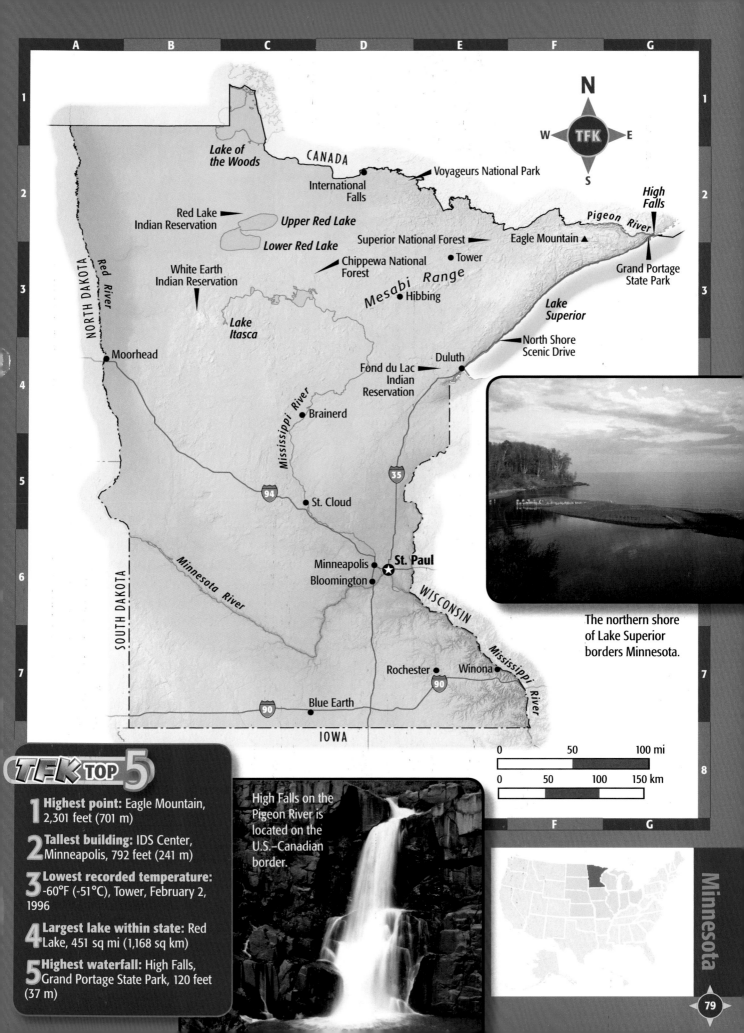

N W **TFK** E S

CANADA

Lake of the Woods

International Falls ▸ Voyageurs National Park

Red Lake Indian Reservation ▸ *Upper Red Lake*

Lower Red Lake

Superior National Forest ▸ Eagle Mountain ▲

High Falls

Pigeon River

Grand Portage State Park

White Earth Indian Reservation ▸

Chippewa National Forest ▸

Mesabi Range

● Tower

● Hibbing

Lake Itasca

Lake Superior

North Shore Scenic Drive ▸

NORTH DAKOTA

Red River

● Moorhead

Fond du Lac Indian Reservation ▸

Duluth

Mississippi River

● Brainerd

35

94

● St. Cloud

SOUTH DAKOTA

Minnesota River

● Minneapolis ★ **St. Paul**

● Bloomington

WISCONSIN

Mississippi River

Rochester ● Winona ●

90

90

● Blue Earth

IOWA

0   50   100 mi
0   50   100   150 km

The northern shore of Lake Superior borders Minnesota.

High Falls on the Pigeon River is located on the U.S.–Canadian border.

TFK TOP 5

1 Highest point: Eagle Mountain, 2,301 feet (701 m)

2 Tallest building: IDS Center, Minneapolis, 792 feet (241 m)

3 Lowest recorded temperature: -60°F (-51°C), Tower, February 2, 1996

4 Largest lake within state: Red Lake, 451 sq mi (1,168 sq km)

5 Highest waterfall: High Falls, Grand Portage State Park, 120 feet (37 m)

Minnesota

Missouri

A bluebird

Independence, **MISSOURI**, was a starting point for many pioneers who headed west on the Oregon and Santa Fe trails in the 1800s. Today, Missouri is where people stop. People come here to see the Gateway Arch in St. Louis. Readers head to Hannibal, the boyhood hometown of Samuel Clemens, better known as Mark Twain. History lovers check out the Pony Express and Jesse James museums in St. Joseph. Missouri's natural beauty is also worth a stop. Tourists enjoy the scenery of the Ozark National Scenic Riverway and Lewis & Clark National Historic Trail.

Large companies also have made a permanent stop in Missouri. They like the fact that Missouri is centrally located in the Midwest (it borders on eight states). Farmers have always found a home in the state. The Missouri River runs west to east through the middle. Above the river are rolling prairies— great for growing soybeans, wheat and corn, as well as for raising cattle. About 100,000 farms are scattered throughout the state. South of the river, the land is rougher, with valleys, cliffs and ridges. Running across the south, the Ozark Plateau is more mountainous and forested. This includes the nine separate parts of the Mark Twain National Forest, which cover 2,343 sq mi (6,068 sq km). It's another great reason to make a stop in Missouri.

THE FACT FILE

Area: 68,898 sq mi (178,446 sq km)

Population: 5,878,415

Capital: Jefferson City

Largest cities (with population):
Kansas City (450,375)
St. Louis (350,759)
Springfield (154,777)

Entered Union (rank):
August 10, 1821 (24)

Motto: *Salus populi suprema lex esto* (The welfare of the people shall be the supreme law)

Tree: flowering dogwood

Flower: hawthorn

Bird: bluebird

Postal code: MO

DID YOU KNOW?

● The Jefferson National Expansion Memorial in St. Louis includes the Gateway Arch, the courthouse that is the site of a ruling on the Dred Scott slavery case and a Museum of Westward Expansion.

● Kansas City has more than 200 fountains, many originally used to water horses. It is claimed that only Rome, Italy, has more fountains.

● Missouri has more than 5,500 caves that have been explored.

Completed in 1965, the Gateway Arch in St. Louis is as wide as it is tall: 630 feet (192 m) in both dimensions.

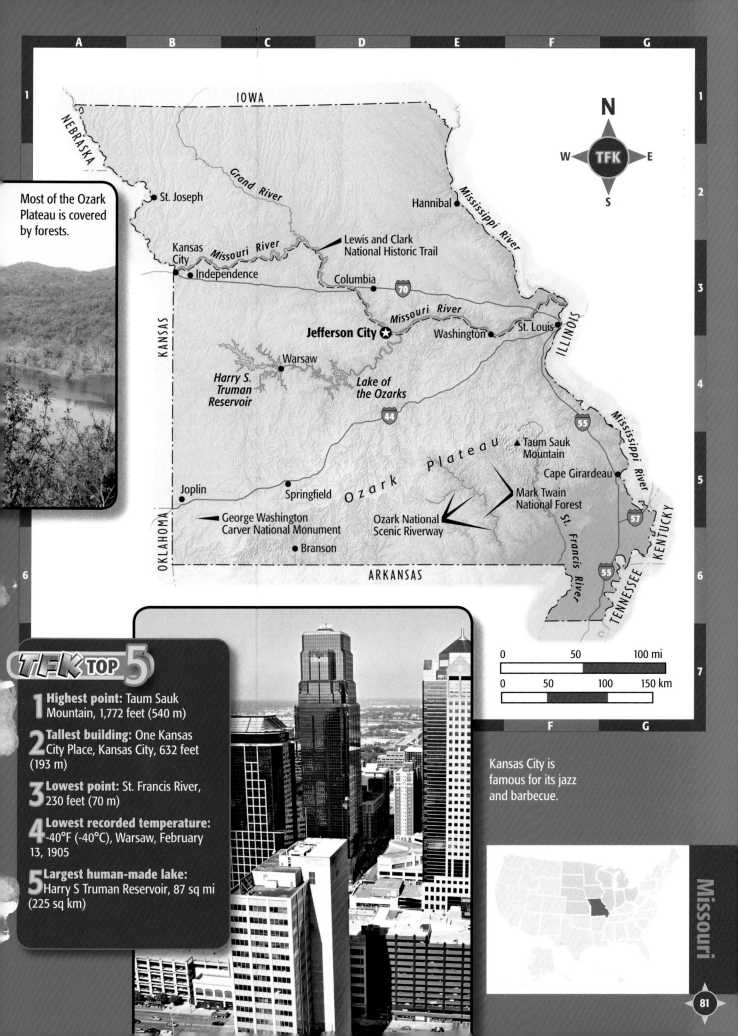

Most of the Ozark Plateau is covered by forests.

IOWA

NEBRASKA

N
W — TFK — E
S

St. Joseph

Grand River

Hannibal

Mississippi River

Kansas City

Missouri River

Independence

Lewis and Clark National Historic Trail

Columbia

70

Jefferson City ☆

Missouri River

Washington

St. Louis

KANSAS

Warsaw

Lake of the Ozarks

Harry S. Truman Reservoir

44

ILLINOIS

55

Taum Sauk Mountain ▲

Joplin

Springfield

Ozark Plateau

Cape Girardeau

Mark Twain National Forest

George Washington Carver National Monument

Ozark National Scenic Riverway

Mississippi River

St. Francis River

57

OKLAHOMA

Branson

55

TENNESSEE

KENTUCKY

ARKANSAS

0   50   100 mi
0   50   100   150 km

TFK TOP 5

1 **Highest point:** Taum Sauk Mountain, 1,772 feet (540 m)

2 **Tallest building:** One Kansas City Place, Kansas City, 632 feet (193 m)

3 **Lowest point:** St. Francis River, 230 feet (70 m)

4 **Lowest recorded temperature:** -40°F (-40°C), Warsaw, February 13, 1905

5 **Largest human-made lake:** Harry S Truman Reservoir, 87 sq mi (225 sq km)

Kansas City is famous for its jazz and barbecue.

Missouri

Nebraska

Explorers in the early 1800s didn't think very much of the land that would become **NEBRASKA**. They called this dry region the Great American Desert. Today, 95 percent of Nebraska is used for farming and ranching, the largest percentage of any state. It is a leading grain producer, especially of corn and wheat. Food grows with the help of irrigation, both from rivers and from the nation's largest underground water supply, the Ogallala Aquifer.

Aside from agriculture, Nebraskans work in telecommunications (especially telemarketing), in manufacturing, and for large insurance companies in Omaha and Lincoln. Meat packing is a major industry in Dakota City and Lexington. Most Nebraskans live in the eastern part of the state, in a geographical area called the Central Lowland. This fertile region makes up one-fifth of the state. The other 80 percent of Nebraska is part of the Great Plains, which is divided between the Sand Hills and the High Plains. The Sand Hills is an area of sand lightly covered by grass that cattle munch on. Winds have pushed the sand into dunes, making it the biggest area of sand dunes in North America. The High Plains is mostly flat grazing land. Nowadays, no one calls Nebraska a "desert"!

THE FACT FILE

Area: 76,878 sq mi (199,113 sq km)

Population: 1,774,571

Capital: Lincoln

Largest cities (with population):
Omaha (424,482)
Lincoln (248,744)
Bellevue (48,391)

Entered Union (rank):
March 1, 1867 (37)

Motto: Equality before the law

Tree: cottonwood

Flower: goldenrod

Bird: western meadowlark

Postal code: NE

DID YOU KNOW?

● In 1986, Nebraska Republican Kay Orr ran against Democrat Helen Boosalis for the office of Governor. It was the first time two women had been candidates for the governorship of any state.

● Ted Turner, the founder of CNN, owns more land than any individual in the state. He bought five large ranches that total more than 666 sq mi (1,719 sq km).

● Monowi, with a population of one, is the smallest incorporated village in Nebraska.

Map

Oglala National Grassland
Pine Ridge
Nebraska National Forest
Sand
Crescent Lake National Wildlife Reserve
● Scottsbluff
North Platte River
Chimney Rock National Historic Site
Lake McConaughy
▲ Panorama Point
80
COLORADO
South Platte R
WYOMING

TFK TOP 5

1 Highest point: Panorama Point, Johnson Township, 5,424 feet (1,653 m)

2 Longest river: Platte River, 310 miles (574 km)

3 Largest human-made lake: Lake McConaughy, 55 sq mi (142 sq km)

4 Lowest point: 840 feet (256 m), at the Missouri River in Richardson County

5 Tallest building: First National Bank Tower, Omaha, 634 feet (193 m)

SOUTH DAKOTA

Niobrara River

Monowi

Missouri River

Niobrara National
Scenic Riverway

Santee Indian
Reservation

Valentine National
Wildlife Refuge

South
Sioux City

Dakota City

Hills

Omaha Indian Reservation

IOWA

Nebraska National Forest

Broken Bow

Platte River

Boys
Town

Omaha
Bellevue

Grand Island

80

Lexington

Kearney

★ Lincoln

MISSOURI

Missouri River

N

W **TFK** E

S

KANSAS

1

2

3

4

5

6

| 0 | 50 | 100 mi |
| 0 | 50 | 100 | 150 km |

The First National
Bank Tower (right)
looms over Omaha.

Chimney Rock was a landmark
for pioneers heading west on the
Oregon Trail in the 1800s. Now a
National Historic Site, it is about
300 feet (91 m) tall.

ROADSIDE FUN

**Stamp collecting can be
a ball.** At least it is in Boys
Town, Nebraska, home
of the world's largest
postage-stamp ball. Boys
Town is both a town and
the home of Boys and Girls
Town—an organization that
helps at-risk kids. In the
1950s, kids there spent six
months sticking together
canceled stamps around
a golf-ball core. Made
of more than 4.5 million
postage stamps, the ball is
32 inches in diameter and
weighs 600 pounds.

Nebraska

North Dakota

NORTH DAKOTA is the most rural state in the nation. Farmland and pastures cover about 80 percent of the land. With rich soil and plenty of sources of water, farmers grow bumper crops of wheat and other grains, such as barley, rye, oats and flax, as well as sunflowers (used to make oil), soybeans and hard beans. Cattle are raised throughout the state, and this contributes to the economy too. Many of North Dakota's farms are located in the fertile Red River Valley, in the east. West of there, the land rises suddenly to form the Drift Prairie, another fertile area covered by fine rock, or drift, that was left by glaciers ages ago. Still farther west is the Great Plains, or Missouri Plateau, vast prairie land where cattle dine on grasses. The Badlands, in the state's southwest corner, is bad land for farming but a fantastic place for gawking at a landscape of unearthly rock formations.

People have come from all over the world to farm this incredibly fruitful land. Many of the first settlers came from Scandinavia and Germany, but over the years, immigrants have arrived here from across the globe. Their descendants continue to produce food from the soil. The many different ethnic celebrations held in North Dakota celebrate the population's diverse heritage.

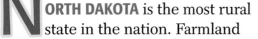
Hundreds of bison roam the Theodore Roosevelt National Park.

THE FACT FILE

Area: 70,704 sq mi (183,123 sq km)

Population: 639,715

Capital: Bismarck

Largest cities (with population):
Fargo (92,660)
Bismarck (59,503)
Grand Forks (51,740)

Entered Union (rank):
November 2, 1889 (39)

Motto: Liberty and union, now and forever: one and inseparable

Tree: American elm

Flower: wild prairie rose

Bird: western meadowlark

Postal code: ND

DID YOU KNOW?

● In 1884, Theodore Roosevelt started the Elkhorn Ranch in North Dakota. The experience made him eager to conserve the environment.

● On November 2, 1889, President Benjamin Harrison signed the two papers that made the states of North and South Dakota. Harrison wouldn't reveal which paper he signed first, so the states entered the Union based on alphabetical order.

● Los Angeles Lakers coach Phil Jackson is from Williston. He played hoops at the University of North Dakota.

North Dakota produces nearly half of the nation's sunflowers.

Williston

Little Missouri National Grassland

MONTANA

Theodore Roosevelt National Park

Badlands

White Butte ▲

Bowman ●

CANADA

● Bottineau

Turtle Mountain
Indian Reservation

1

● Minot

Souris River

Grafton ●

N

W · TFK · E

S

2

Lake
Sakakawea

*Devils
Lake*

Red River

Red River

Fort Berthold
Indian Reservation

Spirit Lake
Indian Reservation

Grand Forks ●

29

Carrington ●

Missouri River

3

James River

MINNESOTA

West Fargo ●

Bismarck

Mandan ● ⭐ **Bismarck**

94

Sheyenne
National Grassland

Fargo

4

Cedar River
National Grassland

Standing Rock
Indian Reservation

Red
River
Valley

29

5

SOUTH DAKOTA

| 0 | 50 | 100 mi |
| 0 | 50 | 100 | 150 km |

TFK TOP 5

1 **Highest point:** White Butte,
3,506 feet (1,069 m)

2 **Longest river:** Red River of the
North, 440 miles (710 km) along the
South Dakota–Minnesota border

3 **Lowest point:** 750 feet (229 m),
at Red River

4 **Largest human-made lake:**
Lake Sakakawea, 536 sq mi
(1,458 sq km)

5 **Tallest building:** North Dakota
State Capitol, Bismarck, 241 feet
(74 m)

The North Dakota
State Capitol can be
seen 20 miles (30 km)
away on a clear day.

North Dakota

Ohio

Grain production is an important part of the Ohio economy.

Ohio makes things. It is third in the U.S. in the number of people with manufacturing jobs. Some of its major cities are industrial centers: Akron is famous for producing rubber, Cincinnati for jet engines, Cleveland for auto parts and steel, Youngstown and Steubenville for steel and Toledo for glass. Lake Erie and the Ohio River make it easy to receive resources and send out finished products. And Ohio has plenty of resources of its own, such as coal, clay, salt beds and oil.

Ohio also grows things. Half the state is farmland, especially northern and western Ohio, where the terrain has been made flat and fertile by ancient glaciers. Top crops include soybeans, corn and wheat. Farms also make money raising sheep and hogs, and from dairy products. Eastern and southeastern Ohio are part of the rugged Appalachian plateau, a land better suited to mining coal than growing food.

But Ohio is more than farms and factories. It has large cities with great attractions, like Cincinnati's National Underground Railroad Freedom Center, Cleveland's Rock and Roll Hall of Fame and Museum and Canton's Pro Football Hall of Fame. Next to Virginia, Ohio has produced the most Presidents—seven—and five of their homes are historic sites.

THE FACT FILE

Area: 40,953 sq mi (106,067 sq km)
Population: 11,466,917
Capital: Columbus
Largest cities (with population):
Columbus (747,755)
Cleveland (438,042)
Cincinnati (332,458)
Entered Union (rank):
March 1, 1803 (17)
Motto: With God all things are possible
Tree: buckeye
Flower: scarlet carnation
Bird: cardinal
Postal code: OH

DID YOU KNOW?

● One of Ohio's state songs is "Hang On Sloopy," a top-40 hit in 1965 that was sung by a local-area pop band called the McCoys. Ohio is the only state with an official rock song.

● The city of Sandusky's Cedar Point Amusement Park has 17 roller coasters, four of them taller than 200 feet (61 m)—both amusement-park records.

● Two great astronauts are from Ohio. In 1962, John Glenn, from Cambridge, was the first American to orbit Earth. In 1969, Wapakoneta native Neil Armstrong became the first person to step on the moon's surface

The Beatles, Elvis Presley and Chuck Berry are among the artists who have been inducted into the Rock and Roll Hall of Fame and Museum, in Cleveland.

ROCK AND ROLL HALL OF FAME AN
ONE K

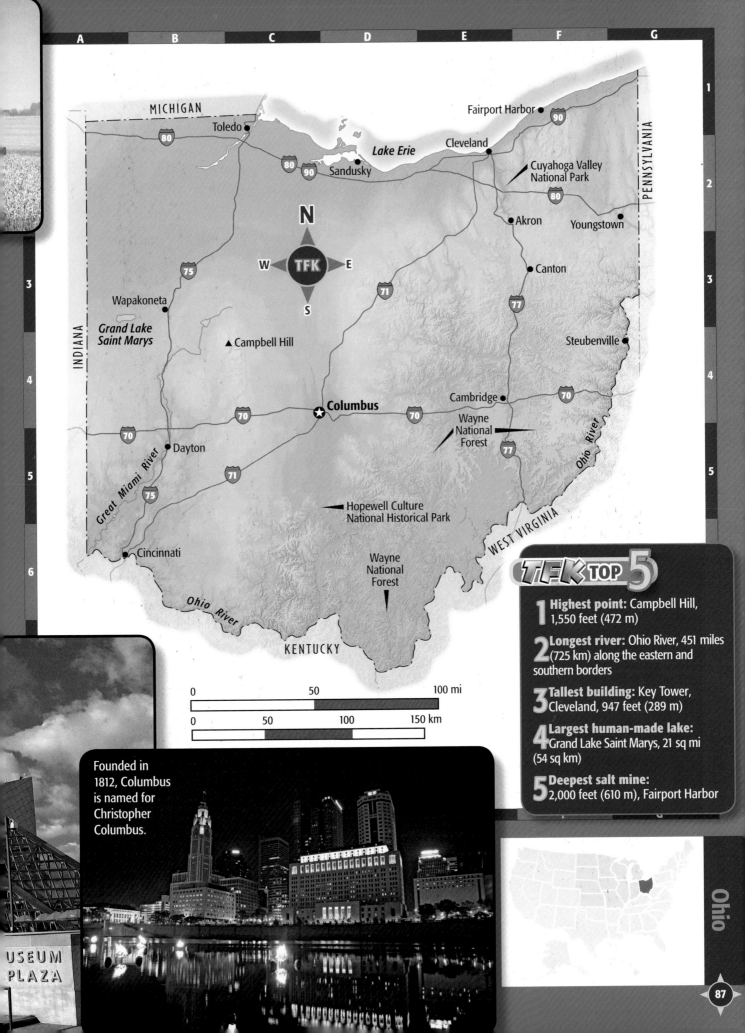

A B C D E F G

1

MICHIGAN

Toledo

Lake Erie

Fairport Harbor 90

Cleveland

Cuyahoga Valley
National Park

80

Sandusky

80
90

Akron

Youngstown

2

PENNSYLVANIA

N

W TFK E

S

Canton

75

Wapakoneta

71

77

3

**Grand Lake
Saint Marys**

▲ Campbell Hill

Steubenville

INDIANA

4

Cambridge

70

70

Columbus

70

Wayne
National
Forest

77

Ohio River

Great Miami River

Dayton

71

75

Hopewell Culture
National Historical Park

5

Cincinnati

Wayne
National
Forest

WEST VIRGINIA

6

Ohio River

KENTUCKY

| 0 | | 50 | | 100 mi |
| 0 | 50 | 100 | 150 km |

TFK TOP 5

1 **Highest point:** Campbell Hill,
1,550 feet (472 m)

2 **Longest river:** Ohio River, 451 miles
(725 km) along the eastern and
southern borders

3 **Tallest building:** Key Tower,
Cleveland, 947 feet (289 m)

4 **Largest human-made lake:**
Grand Lake Saint Marys, 21 sq mi
(54 sq km)

5 **Deepest salt mine:**
2,000 feet (610 m), Fairport Harbor

Founded in
1812, Columbus
is named for
Christopher
Columbus.

MUSEUM
PLAZA

Ohio

South Dakota

T he Mount Rushmore monument is a wonder. Its setting, the Black Hills, is equally wondrous—the peaks were sacred to Indian tribes who lived here. In fact, much of **SOUTH DAKOTA** is pretty special. It's a place that has a wild Wild West history, pleasant cities and varied landscapes.

The state is divided into east and west halves by the Missouri River. East of the Missouri is flat, fertile land dotted with small lakes. It's a great place for growing corn and soybeans. It's also the location of the state's largest cities, which aren't very large.

The land west of the Missouri is mostly part of the Great Plains, a grassy region where cattle and sheep graze. In the southwest corner of the state are the Black Hills and the Badlands National Park.

The whole state attracts businesses, from meat packing to electronics, partly because state taxes are low. About 8.5 percent of South Dakota's population is Native American—the fourth-highest percentage of any state. One-third of western South Dakota is reservation land. South Dakota was also a land of cowboys. The town of Deadwood is a big tourist attraction, because this is where Wild West legends Wild Bill Hickok and Calamity Jane once walked—and drew their guns.

THE FACT FILE

Area: 75,898 sq mi (196,575 sq km)
Population: 796,214
Capital: Pierre
Largest cities (with population):
Sioux Falls (151,505)
Rapid City (63,997)
Aberdeen (24,410)
Entered Union (rank):
November 2, 1889 (40)
Motto: Under God the people rule
Tree: Black Hills spruce
Flower: American pasqueflower
Bird: ring-necked pheasant
Postal code: SD

DID YOU KNOW?

● In 1948, Korczak Ziolkowski began to sculpt the figure of Crazy Horse out of a mountain in the Black Hills. When the Crazy Horse Memorial is finished, it will be 641 feet (195 m) long and 563 feet (171 m) high.

● In 1990, Sue Hendrickson discovered the bones of a *Tyrannosaurus rex* on the Cheyenne River Sioux Reservation. Named Sue, it's the largest, most complete *T-rex* fossil.

● Harney Peak, in the Black Hills, is the highest point in North America east of the Rocky Mountains.

Wind and water erosion formed the strange rocks of the Badlands.

ROADSIDE FUN

The Corn Palace in Mitchell was built in 1921 to celebrate the area's most important crop. The outside of the building is made of plaster, but each year local artists create corny murals that are placed on the inside and outside walls. The murals are made of thousands of bushels of corn, grain, grasses, oats, straw and other crops.

MONTANA

WYOMING

Belle Fo...

Deadwood ●
Mt. R...
Nationa...
Black Hills
Crazy Horse ➤
Memorial

Hot Sprin...

Ch...

MITCHELL CORN PALACE
LIFE ON THE FARM 2005

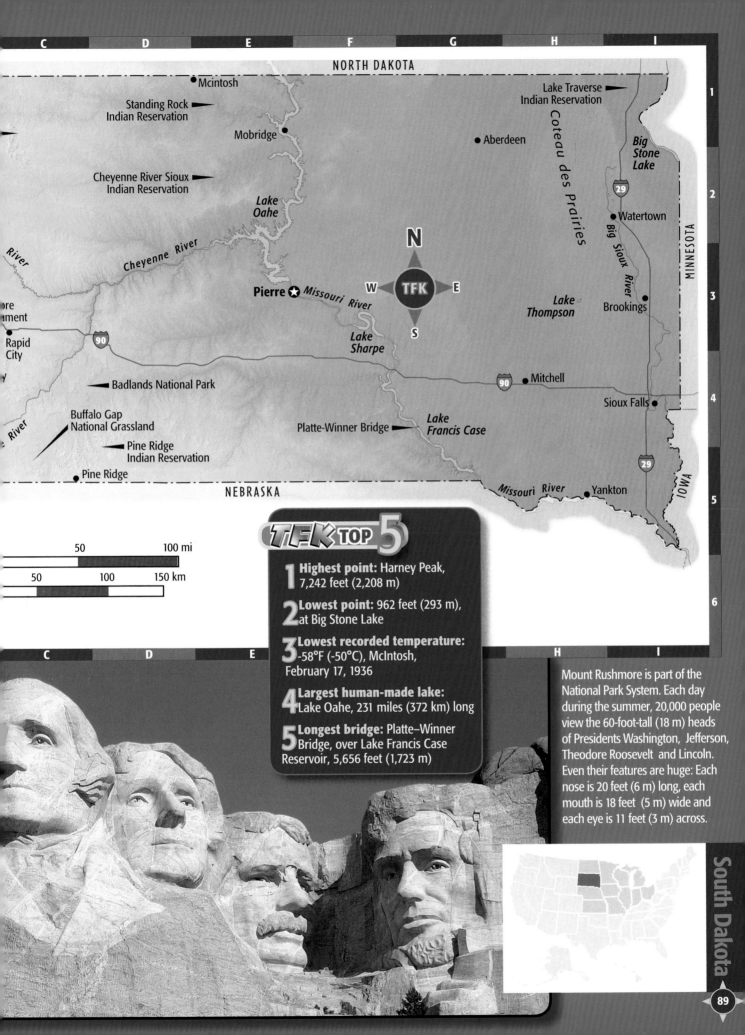

NORTH DAKOTA

Mcintosh

Standing Rock
Indian Reservation

Mobridge

Cheyenne River Sioux
Indian Reservation

Lake
Oahe

Cheyenne River

River

Pierre ⭐ Missouri River

Rapid
City

Badlands National Park

Buffalo Gap
National Grassland

Pine Ridge
Indian Reservation

Pine Ridge

River

NEBRASKA

Lake Traverse
Indian Reservation

Aberdeen

Coteau des prairies

Big
Stone
Lake

Watertown

Big Sioux River

Lake
Thompson

Brookings

MINNESOTA

N
W **TFK** E
S

Lake
Sharpe

Mitchell

Platte-Winner Bridge

Lake
Francis Case

Sioux Falls

Missouri River

Yankton

IOWA

50 **100 mi**

50 **100** **150 km**

TFK TOP 5

1 Highest point: Harney Peak, 7,242 feet (2,208 m)

2 Lowest point: 962 feet (293 m), at Big Stone Lake

3 Lowest recorded temperature: -58°F (-50°C), McIntosh, February 17, 1936

4 Largest human-made lake: Lake Oahe, 231 miles (372 km) long

5 Longest bridge: Platte–Winner Bridge, over Lake Francis Case Reservoir, 5,656 feet (1,723 m)

Mount Rushmore is part of the National Park System. Each day during the summer, 20,000 people view the 60-foot-tall (18 m) heads of Presidents Washington, Jefferson, Theodore Roosevelt and Lincoln. Even their features are huge: Each nose is 20 feet (6 m) long, each mouth is 18 feet (5 m) wide and each eye is 11 feet (3 m) across.

South Dakota

Wisconsin

Lake Michigan forms the state's eastern border.

Cheeseheads—sports fans who wear hats shaped like a wedge of cheese. That's what pops into many people's minds when they think of **WISCONSIN**. True, Wisconsin produces more cheese than any other state. Not to mention that it is second only to California in milk production. But Wisconsin is also an important producer of corn and soybeans, as well as fruits and vegetables. Wisconsinites could also be called cranberry heads. The state produces more of this fruit by far than any other state. Thanks to forests that cover 40 percent of the state, Wisconsin makes more paper products than any other state. Milwaukee is famous for its beer, meat packing is a major industry, and gambling casinos bring in cash on Native American reservations.

Wisconsin also boasts about 15,000 lakes.

Many of them are tucked away in the north, among beautiful forests in a hilly area called the Superior Upland. In the south-central part of the state is the Wisconsin Dells, a gorge on the Wisconsin River known for its incredible rock formations and cliffs. Most of the state's farms, dairy and otherwise, are in the mainly flat plains of the Central Lowlands. This region makes up about two-thirds of the state. Of course, Wisconsin does have cheeseheads, and most of them can be found on Sundays at Lambeau Field in Green Bay, during a Green Bay Packers game.

The Dells of the Wisconsin River has cliffs that are more than 100 feet (30 m) high.

WISCONSIN

1848

THE FACT FILE

Area: 65,498 sq mi (169,639 sq km)
Population: 5,601,640
Capital: Madison
Largest cities (with population):
Milwaukee (602,191)
Madison (228,775)
Green Bay (100,781)
Entered Union (rank):
May 29, 1848 (30)
Motto: Forward
Tree: sugar maple
Flower: wood violet
Bird: robin
Postal code: WI

DID YOU KNOW?

● The world's first power plant to use running water to produce electricity began operation on the Fox River, in Appleton, in 1882.

● The most famous motorcycle made in America, the Harley-Davidson, was created by two friends from Milwaukee, William S. Harley and Arthur Davidson, in the early 1900s.

● The Republican Party got its start in Ripon, in 1854. It was formed to oppose the spread of slavery to new territories. The first Republican candidate for President was John C. Fremont in 1856. The second, in 1860, was Abraham Lincoln.

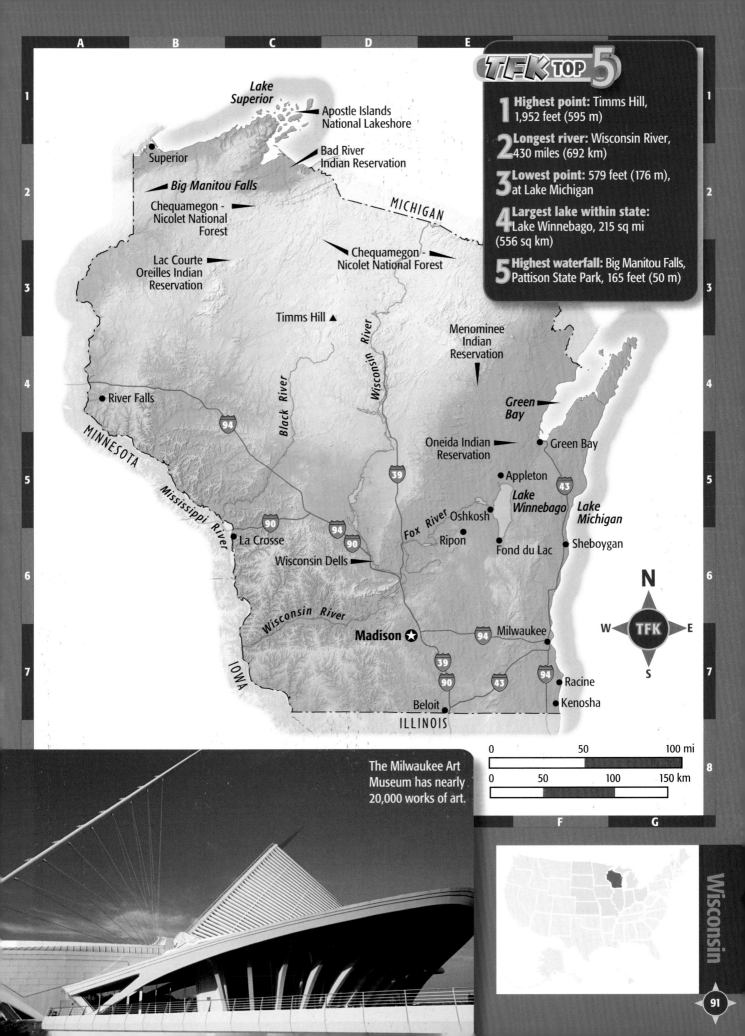

Lake Superior

Apostle Islands National Lakeshore

Superior

Bad River Indian Reservation

Big Manitou Falls

Chequamegon - Nicolet National Forest

MICHIGAN

Lac Courte Oreilles Indian Reservation

Chequamegon - Nicolet National Forest

Timms Hill ▲

Menominee Indian Reservation

Black River

Wisconsin River

River Falls

Green Bay

MINNESOTA

Oneida Indian Reservation

Green Bay

94

Appleton

39

43

Mississippi River

Lake Winnebago

Lake Michigan

Fox River

Oshkosh

90

94

La Crosse

Ripon

90

Fond du Lac

Sheboygan

Wisconsin Dells

Wisconsin River

Madison ★

Milwaukee

94

IOWA

39

94

90

43

94

Racine

Beloit

Kenosha

ILLINOIS

TFK TOP 5

1 Highest point: Timms Hill, 1,952 feet (595 m)

2 Longest river: Wisconsin River, 430 miles (692 km)

3 Lowest point: 579 feet (176 m), at Lake Michigan

4 Largest lake within state: Lake Winnebago, 215 sq mi (556 sq km)

5 Highest waterfall: Big Manitou Falls, Pattison State Park, 165 feet (50 m)

N
W · TFK · E
S

0   50   100 mi

0   50   100   150 km

The Milwaukee Art Museum has nearly 20,000 works of art.

Southwest

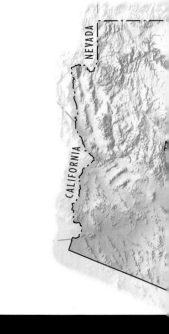

The **SOUTHWEST** is rich in natural resources—from copper in Arizona and silver in New Mexico to oil in Oklahoma and Texas. One valuable resource is scarce: water. Much of the Southwest is arid, but the region's many dams have allowed cities like Phoenix and Albuquerque to take root in deserts. In addition to its stark beauty, the Southwest boasts a fascinating mix of cultures. Native Americans have lived here for thousands of years. Today, Arizona, New Mexico, Oklahoma and Texas all rank among the top 10 states with the highest population of American Indians. More than a quarter of the population of Arizona and a third of the populations of New Mexico and Texas are Hispanic. Points of interest—like the Grand Canyon in Arizona, Carlsbad Caverns in New Mexico, the Johnson Space Center in Texas and the National Cowboy Hall of Fame and Western Heritage Center in Oklahoma—make the Southwest a popular region to visit.

THE FACT FILE

States: Arizona, New Mexico, Oklahoma, Texas

Area: 565,600 sq mi (1,466,972 sq km)

Population: 35,830,366

Highest point: Wheeler Peak, New Mexico, 13,161 ft (4,011 m)

Lowest point: Sea level at the Gulf of Mexico

Largest state: Texas, 261,914 sq mi (678,358 sq km)

Smallest state: Oklahoma, 68,679 sq mi (177,880 sq km)

Most populous state: Texas, 23,904,380

Least populous state: New Mexico, 1,969,915

DID YOU KNOW?

● The Anasazi, or ancestral Pueblo, were the forebears of modern Pueblo Indian tribes of the Southwest. They built stone houses stacked atop each other and dwellings on the sides of cliffs. Their ruins are found in New Mexico and Arizona.

● Texas is bigger than Illinois, Indiana, Ohio, Pennsylvania, New York and West Virginia combined.

● The Four Corners monument marks the spot where the boundaries of Arizona, New Mexico, Utah and Colorado intersect—the only place in the U.S. where four states meet at one point.

COLORADO   KANSAS

MISSOURI

NEW MEXICO   OKLAHOMA

ARKANSAS

NEW MEXICO

TEXAS

MEXICO

Gulf of Mexico

In 1836, Texans
and Mexicans
battled at the
Alamo, in
San Antonio.

N
W TFK E
S

0   50   100 mi

0   50   100   150 km

New Mexico produces the
most chili peppers in the U.S.

Arizona

The Three Sisters rock formation is found in the majestic Monument Valley.

Any list of the world's top tourist attractions would include the Grand Canyon, an astounding valley carved by the Colorado River for 277 miles (446 km). Monument Valley, the Petrified Forest and Hoover Dam are other star **ARIZONA** attractions. Its vast, breathtaking deserts cover about one-third of the state and are home to such unique species as the saguaro cactus, which can grow up to 45 feet (13 m) high, and the Gila monster, which can grow as large as two feet, and is the only poisonous lizard in the U.S.

People once were attracted to Arizona just to make money from mining minerals like copper or to work in military installations. Nowadays, even more people are drawn to its hot, dry climate. Hiking in beautiful wilderness settings and playing golf and tennis under the endlessly sunny skies are favorite activities for tourists and residents alike, as is skiing in the mountains of north central and eastern Arizona. Towns like Tombstone highlight the state's Wild West roots, and the large Native American and Hispanic populations create a fascinating blend of cultures: Arizona has the third-largest number of Native Americans in the U.S., and about 25 percent of the state's population is of Hispanic ancestry.

THE FACT FILE

Area: 113,642 sq mi (294,331 sq km)

Population: 6,338,755

Capital: Phoenix

Largest cities (with population):
Phoenix (1,552,259)
Tucson (525,529)
Mesa (452,933)

Entered Union (rank):
February 14, 1912 (48)

Motto: *Ditat deus* (God enriches)

Tree: Palo verde

Flower: flower of saguaro cactus

Bird: cactus wren

Postal code: AZ

DID YOU KNOW?

● A meteor that crashed into northern Arizona 50,000 years ago created Meteor Crater. It is 4,180 feet (1,275 m) wide and 580 feet (174 m) deep.

● Thieves in Arizona are digging up desert saguaro cactuses and selling them illegally. The National Park Service is putting microchips into cactuses to identify stolen plants.

● According to local legend, the city of Flagstaff got its name from a very tall flagpole settlers used to raise the U.S. flag on July 4, 1876.

The impact of a meteor about 80 feet (24 m) in diameter formed Meteor Crater.

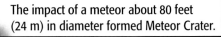

A meteorite found in the crater.

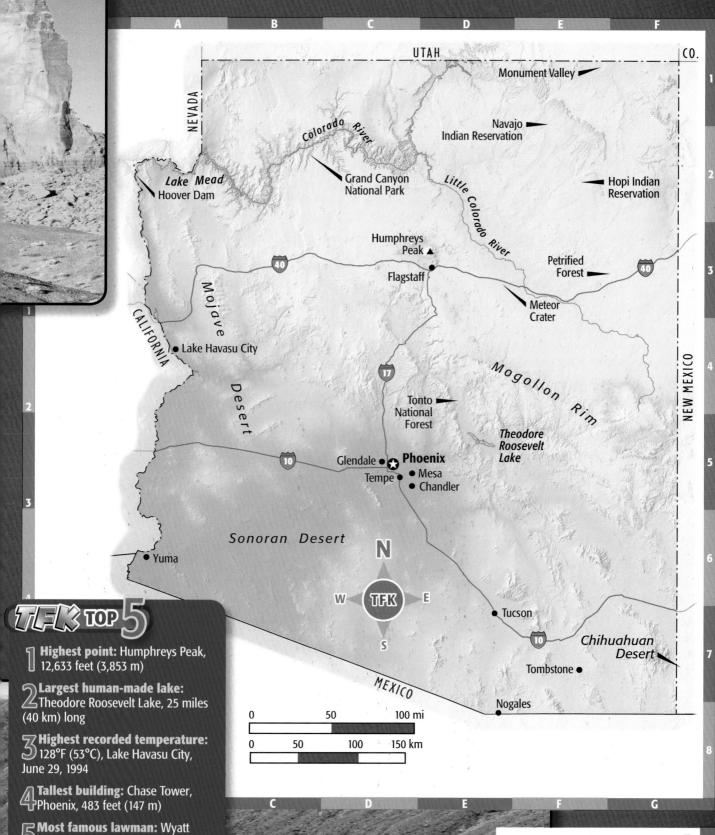

UTAH — CO.

Monument Valley

NEVADA

Colorado River

Navajo
Indian Reservation

Lake Mead
Hoover Dam

Grand Canyon
National Park

Little Colorado River

Hopi Indian
Reservation

Humphreys
Peak ▲

Flagstaff

Petrified
Forest

CALIFORNIA

Mojave

Desert

Lake Havasu City

Meteor
Crater

NEW MEXICO

Mogollon Rim

Tonto
National
Forest

Theodore
Roosevelt
Lake

Glendale • ★ **Phoenix**
Tempe • • Mesa
• Chandler

Sonoran Desert

N

W TFK E

S

Yuma

Tucson

Chihuahuan
Desert

Tombstone •

MEXICO

Nogales •

0   50   100 mi

0   50   100   150 km

TFK TOP 5

1 **Highest point:** Humphreys Peak,
12,633 feet (3,853 m)

2 **Largest human-made lake:**
Theodore Roosevelt Lake, 25 miles
(40 km) long

3 **Highest recorded temperature:**
128°F (53°C), Lake Havasu City,
June 29, 1994

4 **Tallest building:** Chase Tower,
Phoenix, 483 feet (147 m)

5 **Most famous lawman:** Wyatt
Earp (1848–1929), deputy
sheriff of Tombstone

New Mexico

There are three different sections to **NEW MEXICO**'s geography. Eastern New Mexico is part of the Great Plains—grasslands with cattle ranches and horse farms. In southern and south-central New Mexico, the Basin and Range region is composed of valleys between snow-topped, often forested mountains. The third section is the Colorado Plateau in northwestern New Mexico, an area filled with mesas and canyons. The Bisti Badlands—formed by ancient lava flows—are located in the high desert area. New Mexico is rich in minerals like copper, uranium, gold and silver. Despite having to farm on such arid land, New Mexicans raise sheep, grow cotton, and produce more chilies than any other state.

New Mexico's population can also be divided into three main groups: Anglo, Hispanic and Native American. Hispanics make up 44 percent of the population, the highest percentage of Hispanics in any state. Almost 10 percent of the state's population is Native American, the third-highest percentage of any state. About 10 percent of New Mexico is owned by Indian tribes, including the Zuni, Apache and Navajo. They celebrate their heritage with festivals and fairs.

THE FACT FILE

Area: 121,365 sq mi (314,334 sq km)

Population: 1,969,915

Capital: Santa Fe

Largest cities (with population):
Albuquerque (518,271)
Las Cruces (89,722)
Rio Rancho (75,978)

Entered Union (rank):
January 6, 1912 (47)

Motto: *Crescit eundo*
(It grows as it goes)

Tree: piñon

Flower: yucca

Bird: roadrunner

Postal code: NM

DID YOU KNOW?

● Scientists at the Los Alamos National Laboratory in New Mexico created the first atom bomb. It was set off on July 16, 1945, near Alamogordo.

● At 7,000 feet (2,133 m), Santa Fe is the highest capital city in the U.S.

● In 1950, the town of Hot Springs changed its name to Truth or Consequences. That year, the radio show *Truth or Consequences* had promised to broadcast a show from the first town to rename itself after the program.

Erosion created the strange landscape of the Bisti Badlands.

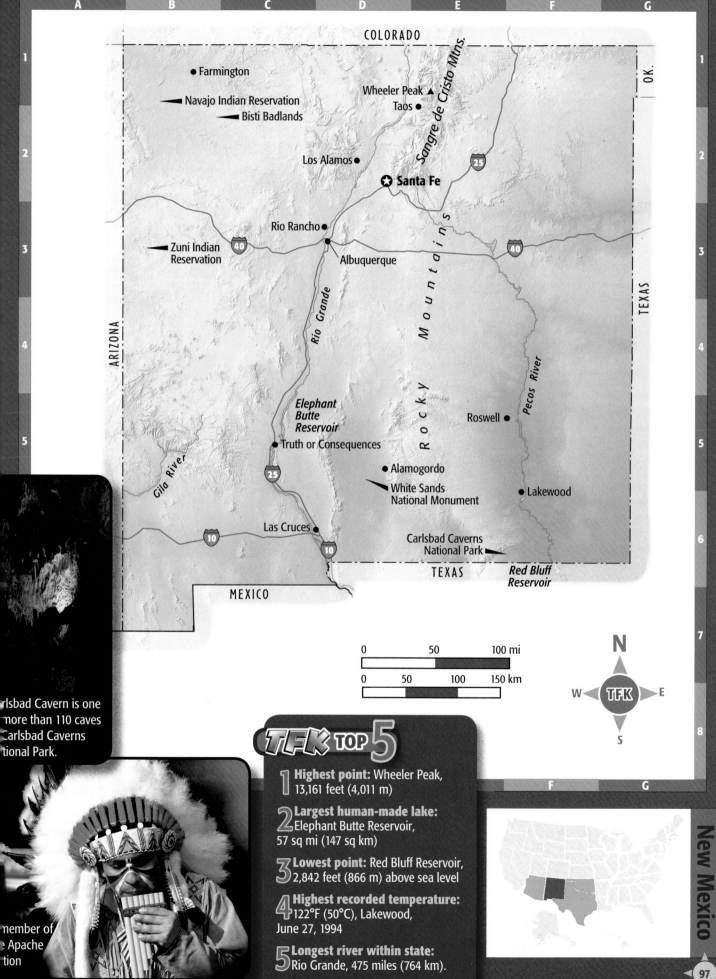

COLORADO

● Farmington

◀ Navajo Indian Reservation
◀ Bisti Badlands

Wheeler Peak ▲
Taos ●

Sangre de Cristo Mtns.

O.K.

Los Alamos ●

⭐ **Santa Fe**

25

Rio Rancho ●

◀ Zuni Indian
Reservation

40

● Albuquerque

40

ARIZONA

Rio Grande

Rocky Mountains

Pecos River

TEXAS

*Elephant
Butte
Reservoir*

Roswell ●

● Truth or Consequences

Gila River

● Alamogordo

◀ White Sands
National Monument

● Lakewood

25

Las Cruces ●

10

Carlsbad Caverns
National Park ◀

10

TEXAS

*Red Bluff
Reservoir*

MEXICO

| 0 | 50 | 100 mi |
| 0 | 50 | 100 150 km |

N
W ◀ TFK ▶ E
S

...rlsbad Cavern is one
...more than 110 caves
...Carlsbad Caverns
...tional Park.

...member of
...e Apache
...tion

New Mexico

Oklahoma

OKLAHOMA's past plays a big part in its present. In the 19th century, many Native Americans were forced to move from other parts of the country to live in what became the Oklahoma Territory. Today, Oklahoma's 394,000 American Indians make up about 8 percent of the state's population. In the 1880s, cowboys brought steers to market in Oklahoma City, and the cattle industry is still important. The cowboy tradition lives on in rodeos and in museums like the National Cowboy Hall of Fame and Western Heritage Center in Oklahoma City. In the early 20th century, Oklahoma was the No. 1 oil producer in the U.S. Although the state is now No. 5, "black gold" still helps its economy.

Oklahoma has high plains, hill country, prairies, mountains, forests and valleys. Oklahoma's climate isn't quite as varied as its land, but its weather can be extreme. The state sits in a part of the U.S. where tornadoes frequently form—Oklahoma averages 53 twisters a year!

THE FACT FILE

Area: 68,679 sq mi (177,880 sq km)
Population: 3,617,316
Capital: Oklahoma City
Largest cities (with population):
Oklahoma City (547,274)
Tulsa (384,037)
Norman (106,707)
Entered Union (rank):
November 16, 1907 (46)
Motto: *Labor omnia vincit* (Labor conquers all things)
Tree: redbud
Flower: Oklahoma rose
Bird: scissor-tailed flycatcher
Postal code: OK

DID YOU KNOW?

● Native American Jim Thorpe, one of America's greatest athletes, was born in the 1880s near the town of Prague. An All-American football player, he won two gold medals in the 1912 Olympics.

● On July 16, 1935, the world's first parking meters were set up in Oklahoma City. Oklahoman Carl C. Magee was the inventor.

● On April 22, 1889, the U.S. government opened what would become Oklahoma Territory to settlers. People who jumped the gun and entered the land sooner than permitted were called "Sooners." The nickname stuck.

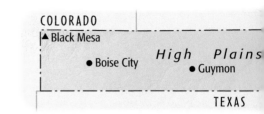

COLORADO
▲ Black Mesa
● Boise City   *High   Plains*
● Guymon
TEXAS

More than 100 rodeos are held every year in Oklahoma. They test a cowpoke's riding skills.

In 1999, a record 145 tornadoes struck Oklahoma.

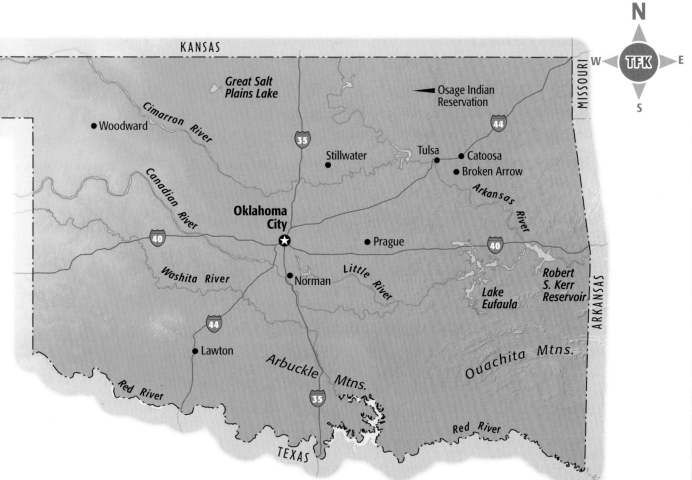

KANSAS

MISSOURI

N
W — **TFK** — E
S

Great Salt
Plains Lake

Osage Indian
Reservation

• Woodward

Cimarron River

35

Stillwater
•

Tulsa • Catoosa
• Broken Arrow

44

Arkansas River

Canadian River

**Oklahoma
City**
★

40

• Prague

40

ARKANSAS

Washita River

Little River

• Norman

Lake
Eufaula

Robert
S. Kerr
Reservoir

44

• Lawton

Arbuckle Mtns.

Ouachita Mtns.

Red River

35

Red River

TEXAS

0   50   100 mi

0   50   100   150 km

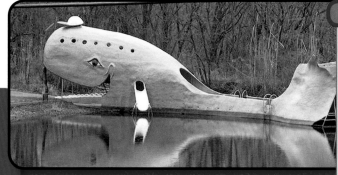

ROADSIDE FUN

It's a whale of a tale:
In the 1970s, a man built a blue whale out of wood, pipe and concrete as an anniversary present to his wife. You can find the 80-foot- (24 m) long "mammal" stranded in a little pond near the town of Catoosa, close to Route 66. Catoosa is not that weird a place to find a beached whale: It is a port city (although it's among the U.S. ports farthest from the sea).

TFK TOP 5

1 Highest point: Black Mesa, 4,973 feet (1,515 m)

2 Biggest human-made lake: Lake Eufaula, 160 sq mi (414 sq km)

3 Lowest point: Little River, 289 feet (88 m)

4 Most populous Native American tribe: Cherokee Nation, 96,519

5 Fastest tornado: 318 mph (512 kph), Oklahoma City, May 3, 1999

Oklahoma's Native American population is second only to that of California.

Oklahoma

Texas

Houston is the largest city in Texas.

The oil industry is big in **TEXAS**. So is raising cotton and cattle. Electronics is also important in the state where the microchip was invented. Just about everything in the Lone Star State is big, starting with its size: Texas is the second-largest state, wide enough to be in both the Central and Mountain time zones. It is second largest in population too.

Texas is the biggest producer of cotton in the U.S. Most of it is grown in the dry west, where irrigation makes farming possible. Along the southern border, where the Rio Grande flows, farmers grow fruits and vegetables. In the central plains, cattle and sheep are raised on huge ranches. And oceans of oil sit under the entire state.

Texas gained its independence from Mexico in 1836, but Mexican influence is still strong in border towns and cities like San Antonio. An independent republic until 1845, Texas entered the Union on its own terms: it did not become a territory before becoming a state. On gaining statehood, it did not give up its public lands to the U.S. government. That Texas spirit of independence lives on today.

THE FACT FILE

Area: 261,914 sq mi (678,358 sq km)
Population: 23,904,380
Capital: Austin
Largest cities (with population):
Houston (2,208,180)
San Antonio (1,328,984)
Dallas (1,240,499)
Entered Union (rank):
December 29, 1845 (28)
Motto: Friendship
Tree: pecan
Flower: bluebonnet
Bird: mockingbird
Postal code: TX

DID YOU KNOW?

● The flags of six different nations have flown over Texas: Spain, France, Mexico, the Republic of Texas, the Confederate States of America and the United States.

● The worst U.S. natural disaster in terms of lives lost took place in Galveston, in 1900. A hurricane flooded the island-city, killing about 8,000 people.

● The King Ranch, near Corpus Christi, is the largest ranch in the U.S. At 1,289 sq mi (3,338 sq km), it is larger than Rhode Island.

Guadalupe Mountains

El Paso

Guadalupe Peak

Rio Grande

ROADSIDE FUN

Among San Antonio's excellent art museums, one truly stands out: **Barney Smith's Toilet Seat Art Museum.** Nearly 700 toilet seats, all painted or engraved by a man named Barney Smith, are on display here. Many have objects glued on them, such as model trains, dog licenses and Boy Scout badges. Smith considers himself an artist who simply uses a different kind of canvas.

Big Tex is the symbol of the annual State Fair of Texas.

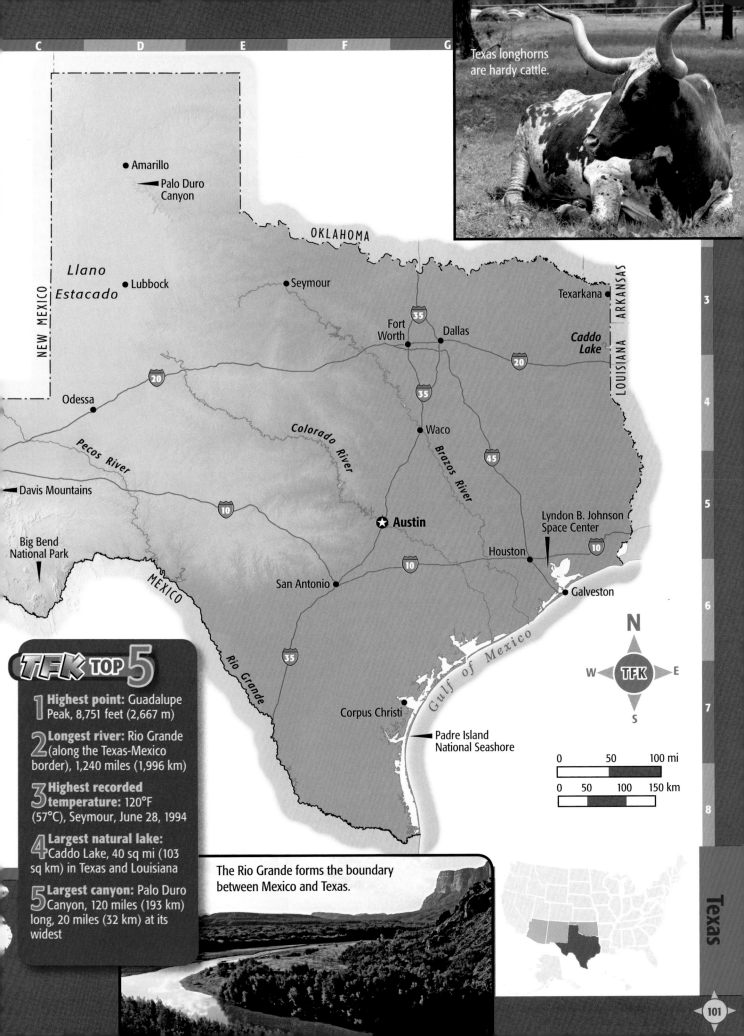

Texas longhorns are hardy cattle.

OKLAHOMA

• Amarillo

◄ Palo Duro Canyon

NEW MEXICO

Llano Estacado

• Lubbock

• Seymour

Texarkana •

ARKANSAS

LOUISIANA

Caddo Lake

Fort Worth • • Dallas

35

20

Odessa •

20

Colorado River

• Waco

Brazos River

45

Pecos River

◄ Davis Mountains

10

★ **Austin**

Lyndon B. Johnson Space Center

10

Big Bend National Park ▼

Houston •

• Galveston

San Antonio •

10

MEXICO

35

Rio Grande

Corpus Christi •

Padre Island National Seashore

Gulf of Mexico

N
W ◄ TFK ► E
S

0   50   100 mi
0   50   100   150 km

TFK TOP 5

1 Highest point: Guadalupe Peak, 8,751 feet (2,667 m)

2 Longest river: Rio Grande (along the Texas-Mexico border), 1,240 miles (1,996 km)

3 Highest recorded temperature: 120°F (57°C), Seymour, June 28, 1994

4 Largest natural lake: Caddo Lake, 40 sq mi (103 sq km) in Texas and Louisiana

5 Largest canyon: Palo Duro Canyon, 120 miles (193 km) long, 20 miles (32 km) at its widest

The Rio Grande forms the boundary between Mexico and Texas.

West

The **WEST** is a region of extremes. The northernmost state, Alaska, reaches the Arctic Circle, while the southernmost continental state, California, borders Mexico. Most Western states are vast in size—seven of the top 10 states in area are in this region—but among the smallest in population.

The West has the nation's highest mountains and some of the lowest points in the U.S. The climate can range from incredibly cold to unbearably hot. Some of the wettest and driest areas are in the West. Amazingly, these extremes can often be found in the same state. What Western states have in common is their abundance of natural wonders—huge wilderness areas with unspoiled forests, fish-filled rivers, deserts, waterfalls, canyons and snowy mountains. Not surprisingly, many monuments and national parks—including Yellowstone—are located in the West.

THE FACT FILE

States: Alaska, California, Colorado, Hawaii, Idaho, Montana, Nevada, Oregon, Utah, Washington, Wyoming
Area: 1,602,521 sq mi (4,150,510 sq km)
Population: 61,788,280
Highest point: Mount McKinley (Denali), Alaska, 20,320 feet (6,194 m)
Lowest point: Death Valley, Badwater, California, 282 ft (86 m) below sea level
Largest state: Alaska: 656,424 sq mi (1,700,135 sq km)
Smallest state: Hawaii: 6,423 sq mi (16,637 sq km)
Most populous state: California: 36,553,215
Least populous State: Wyoming: 522,830
Most populous city: Los Angeles, CA: 3,834,340
Longest river: Colorado River, 1,450 miles (2,333 km)

DID YOU KNOW?

● The most violent volcanic eruption in U.S. history took place on May 18, 1980, when Mount St. Helens, in Washington, blew its top.

● The top 20 tallest peaks in the U.S. are in Alaska, Colorado and California.

● The U.S. government owns about 43% of the land in Western states.

California's Big Sur region has great views of the Pacific Ocean.

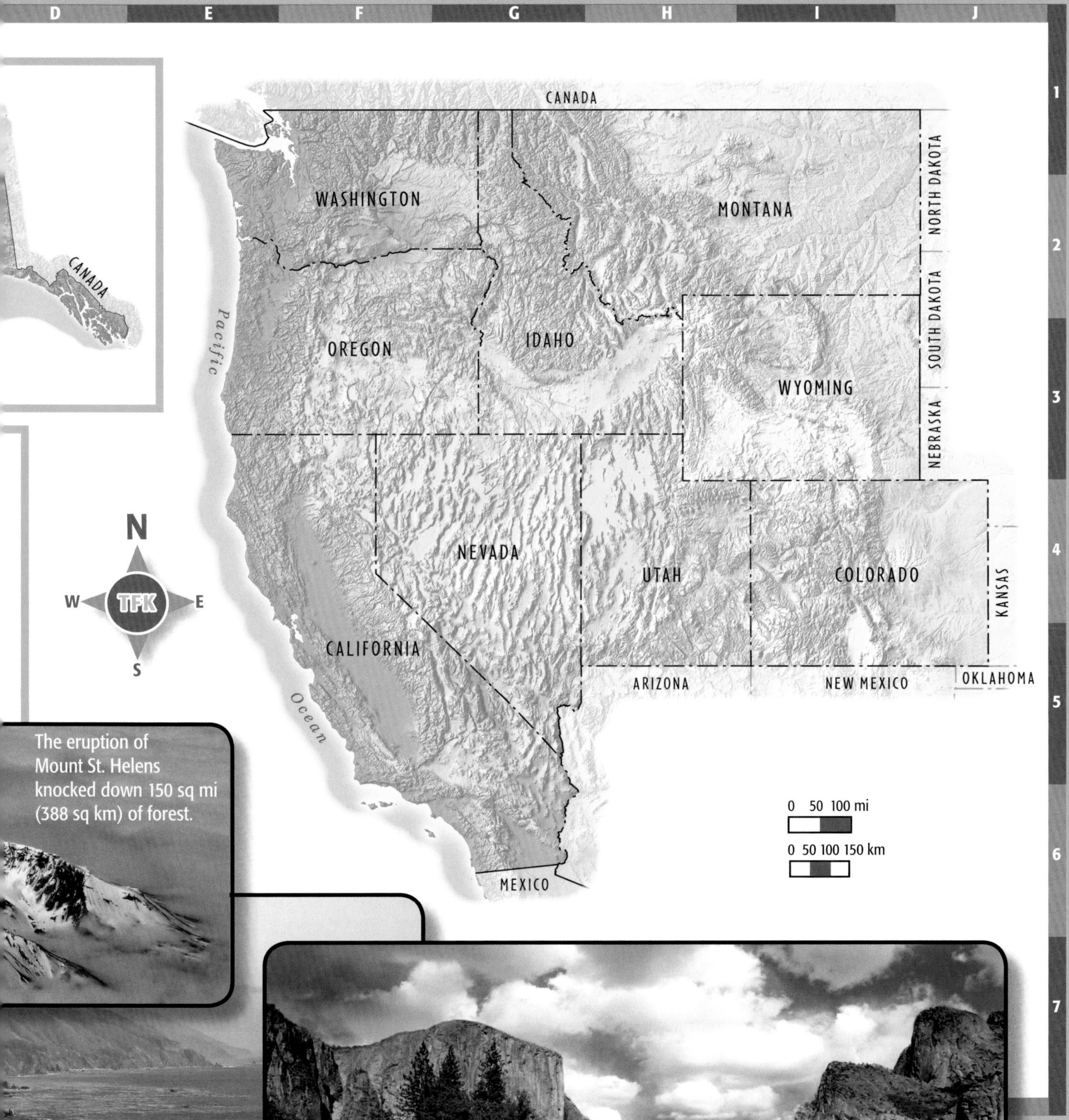
D
E
F
G
H
I
J
1
2
3
4
5
6
7
CANADA
CANADA
WASHINGTON
MONTANA
NORTH DAKOTA
SOUTH DAKOTA
OREGON
IDAHO
WYOMING
NEBRASKA
Pacific
Ocean
N
W
TFK
E
S
NEVADA
UTAH
COLORADO
KANSAS
CALIFORNIA
ARIZONA
NEW MEXICO
OKLAHOMA
MEXICO
0 50 100 mi
0 50 100 150 km

The eruption of Mount St. Helens knocked down 150 sq mi (388 sq km) of forest.

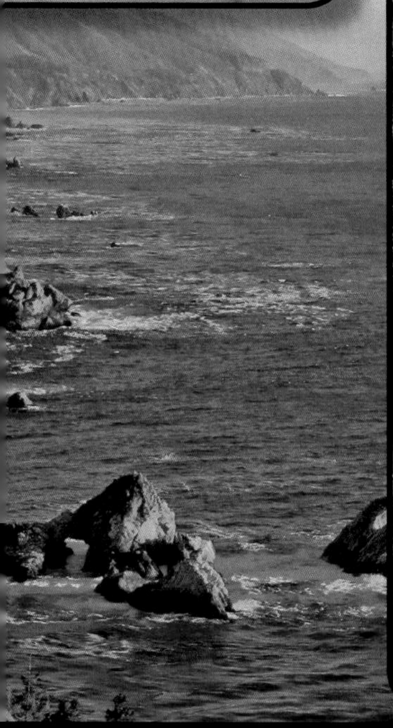

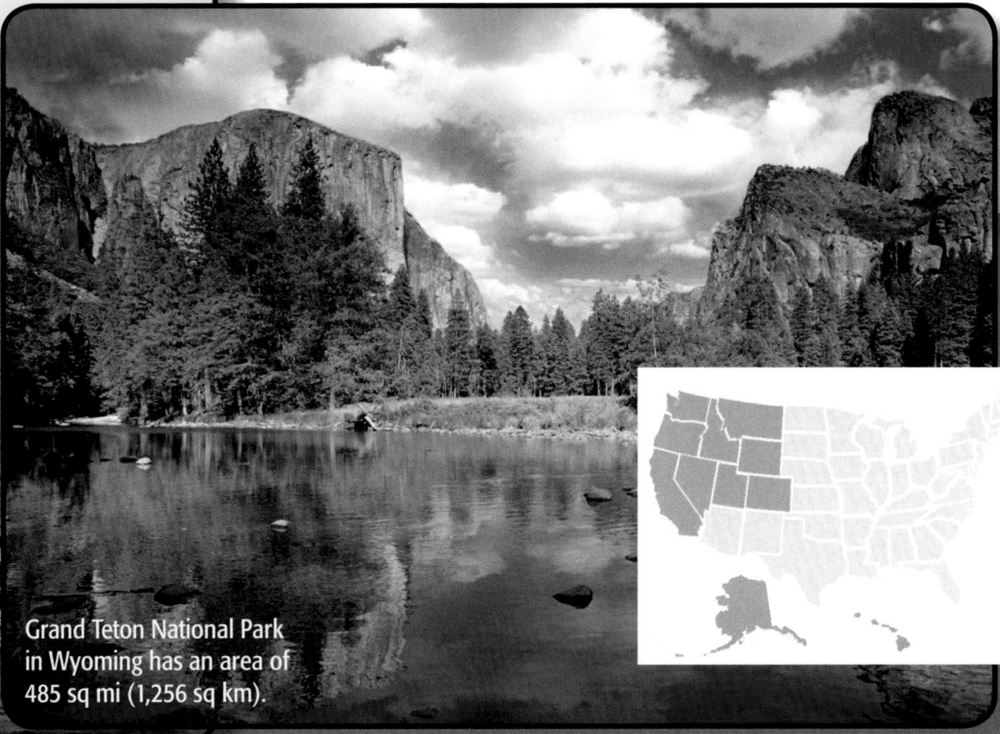

Grand Teton National Park in Wyoming has an area of 485 sq mi (1,256 sq km).

West

Alaska

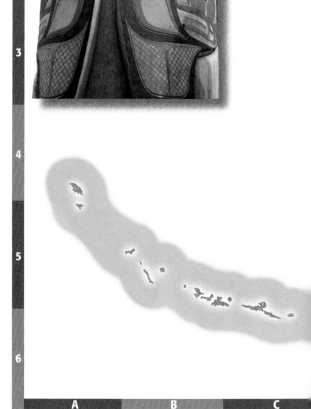

An Alaskan Tlingit Indian carved this totem pole.

T he Native Americans who named **ALASKA** did a good job: Alaska comes from the Aleut word *Alyeska*, meaning "great land." Alaska is just that—the biggest state in the Union. In fact, it has one-sixth of the total land area of the Lower 48 (a term for the continental 48 states). In 1867, when the U.S. bought Alaska from Russia, it got a territory rich in natural resources, especially oil. With its glaciers, lakes, fjords, huge national parks and wildlife refuges, Alaska is also rich in natural beauty. Most Alaskans live in the southern part of the state, south of the Alaska Range. Only the hardiest people live in the far north, inside the Arctic Circle. In Fairbanks, the northernmost major city, winter lasts from September to April, and the average low temperature in January is -19°F (-28°C).

THE FACT FILE

Area: 656,424 sq mi
(1,700,135 sq km)
Population: 683,478
Capital: Juneau
Largest cities (with population):
Anchorage (279,671)
Fairbanks (34,540)
Juneau (30,690)
Entered Union (rank):
January 3, 1959 (49)
Motto: North to the future
Tree: Sitka spruce
Flower: forget-me-not
Bird: willow ptarmigan
Postal code: AK

DID YOU KNOW?

● The annual Iditarod Trail Sled Dog Race pits mushers (riders) and their dog teams in a race from Anchorage to Nome. The brutal 1,150-mile (1,850 km) competition takes 10 to 17 days.

● The Alaska flag was designed by a 13-year-old Aleut from Chignik. Benny Benson, a seventh-grader, entered a contest in 1927 that asked students to design a flag for the Alaska Territory. Benny's winning entry shows the Big Dipper and the North Star, which symbolizes Alaska.

● About 25 percent of the oil produced by the U.S. comes from Alaska.

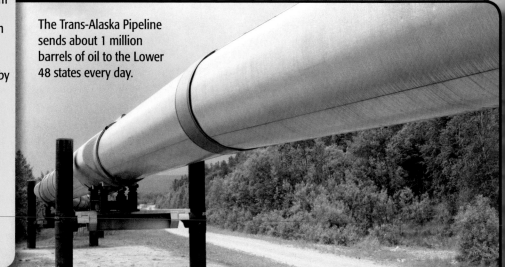

The Trans-Alaska Pipeline sends about 1 million barrels of oil to the Lower 48 states every day.

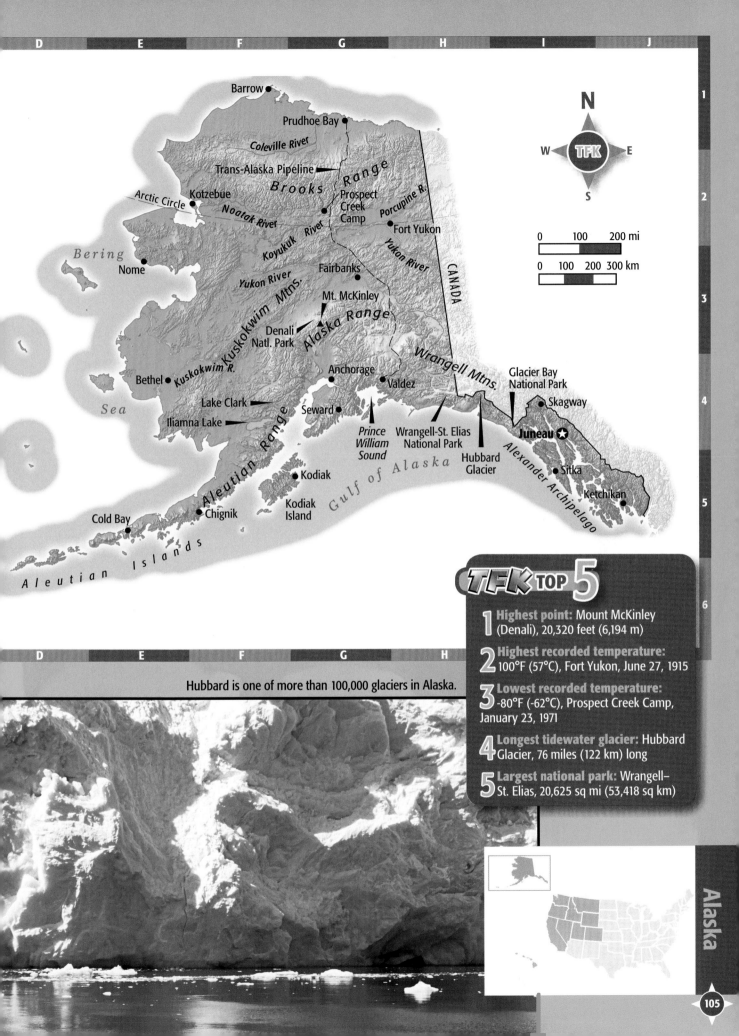

Barrow

Prudhoe Bay

Coleville River

Trans-Alaska Pipeline

Brooks Range

Arctic Circle

Kotzebue

Noatak River

Prospect Creek Camp

Porcupine R.

Koyukuk River

Fort Yukon

Yukon River

CANADA

Bering

Nome

Yukon River

Kuskokwim Mtns.

Fairbanks

Mt. McKinley

Denali Natl. Park

Alaska Range

Wrangell Mtns.

Bethel *Kuskokwim R.*

Anchorage

Valdez

Glacier Bay National Park

Sea

Lake Clark

Seward

Prince William Sound

Wrangell-St. Elias National Park

Hubbard Glacier

Skagway

Juneau ☆

Alexander Archipelago

Iliamna Lake

Aleutian Range

Kodiak

Gulf of Alaska

Sitka

Kodiak Island

Ketchikan

Cold Bay

Chignik

Aleutian Islands

N
W — TFK — E
S

| 0 | 100 | 200 mi |
| 0 | 100 | 200 | 300 km |

3

4

5

6

Hubbard is one of more than 100,000 glaciers in Alaska.

TFK TOP 5

1 Highest point: Mount McKinley (Denali), 20,320 feet (6,194 m)

2 Highest recorded temperature: 100°F (57°C), Fort Yukon, June 27, 1915

3 Lowest recorded temperature: -80°F (-62°C), Prospect Creek Camp, January 23, 1971

4 Longest tidewater glacier: Hubbard Glacier, 76 miles (122 km) long

5 Largest national park: Wrangell– St. Elias, 20,625 sq mi (53,418 sq km)

Alaska

California

CALIFORNIA has great cities, beautiful beaches and amazing redwood forests and is home to such attractions as Disneyland and the San Diego Zoo. That's why California attracts more tourists than any other state. California also has the largest population of any state. About one in every eight Americans lives in California, attracted by an economy that is the largest in the U.S. If California were a country, it would have the seventh largest economy of any nation. Agriculture brings in much of the state's wealth. Silicon Valley, located just north of San Jose, is the heart of the nation's computer and technology industries. And Los Angeles is the center of the movie and TV industries.

California is very long—about 800 miles (1,287 km) from North to South—so it has two different climates. Northern California is cool and wet, while Southern California is warm and dry. North or south, California is a great place to visit—and to live in.

A California sea lion

THE FACT FILE

Area: 155,973 sq mi (403,970 sq km)

Population: 36,553,215

Capital: Sacramento

Largest cities (with population):
Los Angeles (3,834,340)
San Diego (1,336,865)
San Jose (989,486)

Entered Union (rank):
September 9, 1850 (31)

Motto: Eureka (I have found it)

Tree: California redwood

Flower: golden poppy

Bird: California valley quail

Postal code: CA

DID YOU KNOW?

● Skateboarding began in California in the 1950s. Kids there figured out how to surf the sidewalks when there were no waves at the beach: They attached roller-skate wheels to wooden boxes, boards and planks.

● Scientists detect about 500,000 harmless tremors in California from mini-earthquakes every year.

● Inyo National Forest is home to the bristlecone pine, the longest-lived species known. Scientists think some of these trees are more than 4,600 years old.

ROADSIDE FUN

E.T., don't call home—call Lathrop, California. That's where a unique UFO seems to have landed.
The 30-foot (9 m) long flying saucer looks like it crashed into the roof of a convenience store called Tower Mart. There are even little green aliens (models, of course) in the saucer and buying stuff in the store. All of that makes shopping there an out-of-this-world experience.

Mount Whitney is the highest point in the Lower 48 states.

OREGON

▲ Mt. Shasta

Redwood
National
Park

Eureka ●

● Redding

395

5

Sierra Nevada Mountains

Coast Range Mtns.

Sacramento R.

101

1

80

Lake Tahoe

☆ **Sacramento**

Santa Rosa ●

80

Stockton ●
Lathrop

Yosemite National Park

Mono Lake

NEVADA

San Francisco ●
● Berkeley

San ● Jose

Silicon Valley

San Joaquin R.

395

Inyo National Forest

Death Valley National Park

Santa Cruz ●

Monterey ●

101

● Fresno

Sequoia
Natl. Park

▲ Mt. Whitney

Pacific

Ocean

Coast Range Mtns.

1

5

Mojave
National
Preserve

San Luis Obispo ●

● Bakersfield

15

Barstow ●

40

Santa Barbara ●

101

Los
Angeles ●

San Bernardino ●

Palm Springs ●

Santa
Monica ●

1

● Anaheim

10

ARIZONA

*Salton
Sea*

Channel Islands

15

5

San Diego ●

MEXICO

W — **TFK** — E
N / S (compass)

0   50   100 miles

0   50   100   150 kilometers

TFK TOP 5

1 **Highest point:** Mount Whitney, 14,494 feet (4,418 m)

2 **Longest river:** Sacramento River, 382 miles (615 km)

3 **Lowest point:** Death Valley, 282 feet (86 m) below sea level

4 **Highest recorded temperature:** 134°F (57°C), Death Valley, July 10, 1913

5 **Tallest living thing:** a redwood tree in Tall Trees Grove, in Redwood National Park, 368 feet (112 m)

California

Colorado

COLORADO has an average altitude of 6,800 feet (2,072 m), the highest of any state. Fifty-six peaks in Colorado rise above 14,000 feet (4,267 m). People come to ski and snowboard down the snow-covered mountains. They stay at such popular ski resorts as Aspen, Telluride and Vail. More money is brought to Colorado by tourism than by any other industry.

Although the southern part of the Rocky Mountains runs down the middle of Colorado, much of the land on either side is flat. Here you can find grazing land for sheep, as well as farms that grow sugar beets, corn and other crops. Most of Colorado's cities are just east of the Rockies. Denver, the Mile-High City, is 5,280 feet (1,603 m) above sea level. Denverites enjoy its 205 parks that cover 31 sq mi (80 sq km). That shouldn't be surprising, since Coloradans love the outdoors. Hiking, jogging and skiing are among their favorite activities. That's a major reason Colorado has the lowest obesity rate of any U.S. state.

THE FACT FILE

Area: 103,730 sq mi (268,660 sq km)
Population: 4,861,515
Capital: Denver
Largest cities (with population):
Denver (588,349)
Colorado Springs (376,427)
Aurora (311,794)
Entered Union (rank):
August 1, 1876 (38)
Motto: *Nil sine numine* (Nothing without providence)
Tree: Colorado blue spruce
Flower: Rocky Mountain columbine
Bird: lark bunting
Postal code: CO

DID YOU KNOW?

● The song "America the Beautiful" was written in 1893 by Katharine Lee Bates. She was inspired by the view from Pikes Peak, a 14,110-foot (4,300 m) tall mountain near Colorado Springs.

● Colorado's lowest point—3,315 feet (1,010 m)—is higher than any other state's lowest point.

● The tallest sand dunes in the U.S. are found at the Great Sand Dunes National Monument. The tallest of them all, the Star Dune, is 750 feet (228 m) high.

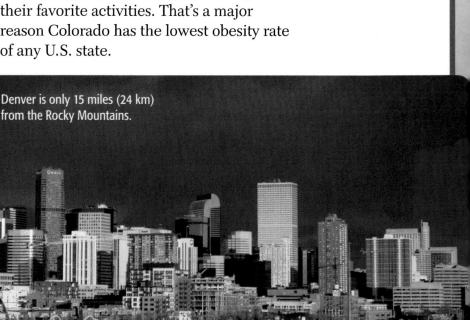

Denver is only 15 miles (24 km) from the Rocky Mountains.

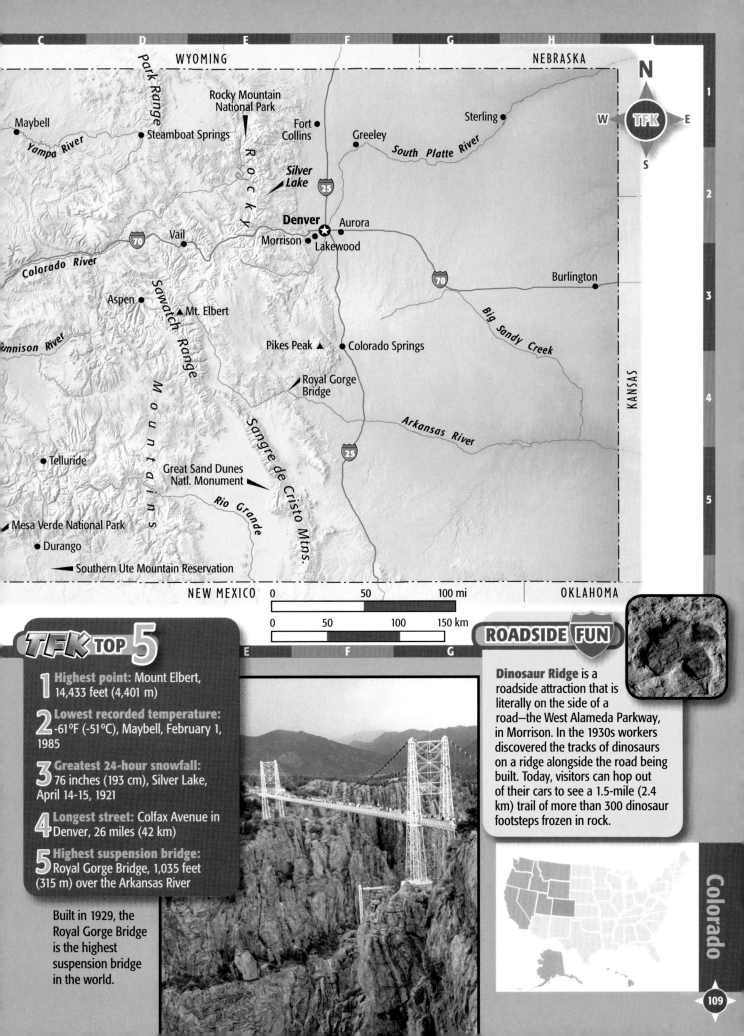

Map Labels

C D E F G H I

WYOMING

NEBRASKA

N
W — TFK — E
S

1

Maybell

Rocky Mountain National Park

Fort Collins

Sterling

Steamboat Springs

Greeley

Yampa River

South Platte River

Park Range

R o c k y

Silver Lake

25

2

Vail

70

Denver

Aurora

Morrison

Lakewood

70

Burlington

Colorado River

Sawatch Range

Aspen

▲ Mt. Elbert

Big Sandy Creek

3

Gunnison River

Pikes Peak ▲

Colorado Springs

Royal Gorge Bridge

M o u n t a i n s

Arkansas River

KANSAS

4

Telluride

25

Great Sand Dunes Natl. Monument

Sangre de Cristo Mtns.

Rio Grande

5

Mesa Verde National Park

Durango

Southern Ute Mountain Reservation

NEW MEXICO   0   50   100 mi
0   50   100   150 km

OKLAHOMA

D E F G

TFK TOP 5

1 Highest point: Mount Elbert, 14,433 feet (4,401 m)

2 Lowest recorded temperature: -61°F (-51°C), Maybell, February 1, 1985

3 Greatest 24-hour snowfall: 76 inches (193 cm), Silver Lake, April 14-15, 1921

4 Longest street: Colfax Avenue in Denver, 26 miles (42 km)

5 Highest suspension bridge: Royal Gorge Bridge, 1,035 feet (315 m) over the Arkansas River

Built in 1929, the Royal Gorge Bridge is the highest suspension bridge in the world.

ROADSIDE FUN

Dinosaur Ridge is a roadside attraction that is literally on the side of a road—the West Alameda Parkway, in Morrison. In the 1930s workers discovered the tracks of dinosaurs on a ridge alongside the road being built. Today, visitors can hop out of their cars to see a 1.5-mile (2.4 km) trail of more than 300 dinosaur footsteps frozen in rock.

Colorado

109

Hawaii

Surfing is popular in Hawaii.

HAWAII is a group of more than 100 islands and atolls, only eight of them inhabited, that stretch over 1,860 miles (3,000 km) of the Pacific Ocean. The islands were formed millions of years ago by an undersea volcano known as a hot spot. The hot spot poured out lava, creating mountains that grew in height until they reached the ocean's surface. The islands are the volcanoes' tops.

There is no other state quite like Hawaii. First, it is located far from the U.S. mainland—2,093 miles (3,364 km). It is the only state that's completely surrounded by water. It has two official languages: English and Hawaiian. It is the only state with a royal palace, the Iolani Palace in Honolulu, built in 1882 for a Hawaiian king. With its warm weather, sandy beaches and lush tropical scenery, Hawaii is a popular tourist destination. One main attraction is Kilauea on the big island of Hawaii. Kilauea is among the most active volcanoes in the world. Lava has been pouring out of it steadily, slowly adding land to the island. That makes Hawaii special in one more way: it is the only state that keeps growing in area.

THE FACT FILE

Area: 6,423 sq mi (16,637 sq km)
Population: 1,283,388
Capital: Honolulu (Oahu)
Largest cities (with population):
Honolulu (375,571)
Hilo (40,759)
Kailua (36,513)
Entered Union (rank):
August 21, 1959 (50)
Motto: *Ua mau ke ea o ka aina i ka pono* (The life of the land is perpetuated in righteousness)
Tree: kukui (candlenut)
Flower: yellow hibiscus (*pua ma'o hau hele*)
Bird: nene (Hawaiian goose)
Postal code: HI

DID YOU KNOW?

● On December 7, 1941, Japanese planes attacked U.S. ships in Pearl Harbor, on the island of Oahu. The next day, the U.S. declared war on Japan.

● Polynesians brought body surfing to Hawaii as early as the 4th century. Later, Hawaiians started riding upright on long boards.

● Mauna Kea is the tallest mountain in the Pacific. Counting the part of it below the ocean's surface, it is the tallest mountain in the world—a total of 33,796 feet (10,205 m).

Kilauea has been erupting nonstop since 1983.

Pearl Harbor is the base for the U.S. Pacific Fleet.

Pacific

OAHU
Pearl City
Waipahu
Pearl Harbor
Kaneohe
Kailua
★ **Honolulu**

MOLOKAI
Kaunakakai

Garden of the Gods
Lanai City •

LANAI

MAUI
Wailuku
Kahului •
Kihei
Haleakala National Park

KAHOOLAWE

Ocean

HAWAII
• Waimea
Mauna Kea ▲
Hilo •
Wailuku R.
Kailua-kona •
▲ Kilauea
Hawaii Volcanoes National Park
Pahala •
Ka Lae •

N
W — TFK — E
S

| 0 | 50 | 100 mi |
| 0 | 50 | 100 | 150 km |

At the top of Mauna Kea is one of the world's biggest observatories.

TFK TOP 5

1 Highest point: Mauna Kea, Hawaii, 13,796 feet (4,205 m)

2 Largest island: Hawaii, 4,038 sq mi (10,458 sq km)

3 Smallest inhabited island: Lanai, 141 sq mi (365 sq km)

4 Highest recorded temperature: 100°F (38°C), Pahala, April 27, 1931

5 Wettest spot: Mount Waialeale, averages 488 inches (1,239 cm) of rain yearly

The Garden of the Gods, on Lanai, is an unusual rock formation.

Hawaii

Idaho

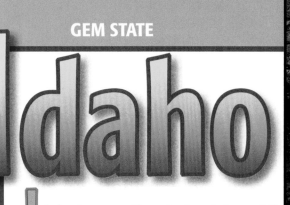

The Perrine Bridge stands 486 feet (148 m) above the Snake River.

Idaho is more than just potatoes. Of course, potatoes *are* important to Idaho, as the state produces one-third of all U.S. spuds, more than any other state. But these tasty tubers are grown only in the Snake River Plain, a small area in the south-central part of the state. This is the only flat area of the state, and it is here that most towns and cities are located. The rest of Idaho is covered by mountains and thick forests. The northern part of the state, called the Panhandle, is almost unspoiled territory.

The state's untouched beauty is as important as its potatoes. Tourists and residents alike enjoy white-water rafting on the Salmon and Clearwater rivers, as well as camping and hiking in the state's 28,125 sq mi (72,843 sq km) of wilderness. The endless lakes and rivers are perfect for catching rainbow trout. Many people ski in Sun Valley and other resorts. One of Idaho's most amazing spots is the Craters of the Moon National Monument. Ancient volcanoes created an unearthly landscape that looks like the surface of the moon. That's why NASA once trained astronauts there.

THE FACT FILE

Area: 82,751 sq mi (214,325 sq km)
Population: 1,499,402
Capital: Boise
Largest cities (with population):
Boise (202,832)
Nampa (79,249)
Meridian (64,642)
Entered Union (rank):
July 3, 1890 (43)
Motto: *Esto perpetua* (It is forever)
Tree: white pine
Flower: syringa
Bird: mountain bluebird
Postal code: ID

DID YOU KNOW?

● Mining lobbyist George M. Willing chose the state's name. He claimed Idaho was an Indian word meaning "gem of the mountains." Willing had made up the name, but it stuck.

● The world's first ski lift was built in Sun Valley in 1936. Its design was based on a device that lifted bananas into boats.

● Idaho has more wilderness area than any other state in the continental U.S.

TFK TOP 5

1. **Highest point:** Borah Peak, 12,662 feet (3,859 m)

2. **Deepest river canyon:** Hells Canyon, 7,993 feet (2,436 m)

3. **Longest river:** Snake river, 490 miles (790 km)

4. **Largest lake:** Pend Oreille, 133 sq mi (344 sq km)

5. **Largest tree:** Champion Western Red Cedar tree, Elk River, 177 feet (54 m) high, 18 feet (5 m) in diameter

Ancient lava flows created the eerie landscape of the Craters of the Moon National Monument.

CANADA

B C D E F G

WASHINGTON

Sandpoint

Lake Pend Oreille

Coeur
d'Alene

90

Coeur d'Alene
Reservation

Bitterroot Range

Elk River
Moscow

Clearwater River

Nez Perce
Reservation

*Clearwater
Mountains*

Grangeville

MONTANA

Salmon River

Hells Canyon

Salmon

*Salmon
River
Mountains*

Bitterroot Range

Snake River

▲ Borah Peak

Yellowstone
Natl. Park

15

N
W E
S
TFK

Sun Valley

Craters of the
Moon Natl. Park

OREGON

Meridian
★ Boise
Nampa

Ketchum
Hailey

Snake River Plain

Idaho
Falls

WYOMING

Fort Hall
Reservation

0   50   100 mi
0   50   100   150 km

84

Perrine
Bridge

*American Falls
Reservoir*

Snake River

Pocatello

Twin Falls

Preston

NEVADA

UTAH

The Clearwater River is known as a great
place to fish for steelhead and salmon.

Idaho spuds

E

Montana

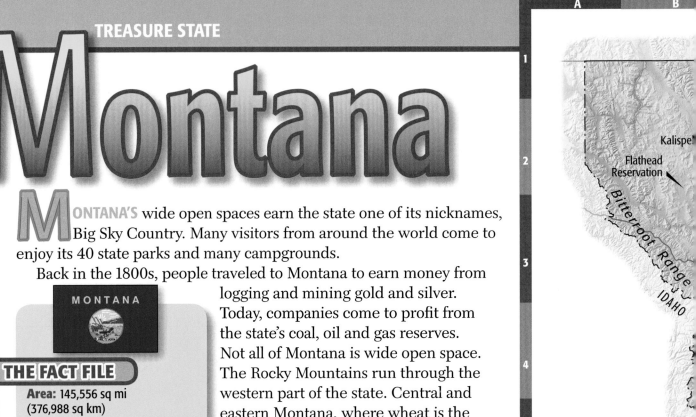

ONTANA'S wide open spaces earn the state one of its nicknames, Big Sky Country. Many visitors from around the world come to enjoy its 40 state parks and many campgrounds.

Back in the 1800s, people traveled to Montana to earn money from logging and mining gold and silver. Today, companies come to profit from the state's coal, oil and gas reserves. Not all of Montana is wide open space. The Rocky Mountains run through the western part of the state. Central and eastern Montana, where wheat is the main crop, are part of the Great Plains. Most Montanans live closer to the mountains. But even the crowded part of Montana isn't very crowded, with six people per square mile. Those people include Native Americans, who as the first settlers have played a large part in the state's history. Today, there are members of as many as 11 different tribes and seven Native American reservations.

THE FACT FILE

Area: 145,556 sq mi
(376,988 sq km)
Population: 957,861
Capital: Helena
Largest cities (with population):
Billings (101,876)
Missoula (67,165)
Great Falls (58,827)
Entered Union (rank):
November 8, 1889 (41)
Motto: *Oro y plata*
(Gold and silver)
Tree: Ponderosa pine
Flower: bitterroot
Bird: western meadowlark
Postal code: MT

DID YOU KNOW?

● The first female congresswoman, Jeannette Rankin, came from Montana. She was elected to the U.S. House of Representatives in 1916.

● Montana is the only state where water from its rivers flows to the Pacific Ocean, Atlantic Ocean and Arctic Ocean (through Hudson Bay in Canada).

● The town of Browning holds the record for the greatest temperature change in a 24-hour period. From January 23 to January 24, the temperature changed 100°F (56°C), dropping from 44°F (7°C) to -56°F (-49°C).

Montana has more grizzly bears than any other state in the Lower 48.

The sky looks big above wide open Montana prairies.

CANADA

Blackfeet Reservation

• Browning
Glacier National
Park

• Shelby

• Havre

Fort Peck
Reservation

Rocky

Flathead Lake

Giant Springs

Fort Belknap
Reservation

Wolf Point

Missouri River

Missoula

Missouri River

Fort Peck Lake

NORTH DAKOTA

• Glendive

Roe River
Great Falls

Helena ✪

Anaconda •

• Butte

Bozeman •

Musselshell River

Yellowstone River

Fort Keogh

Billings •

SOUTH DAKOTA

Mountains

Bitterroot

Yellowstone National Park

▲Granite Peak

WYOMING

Range

N
W TFK E
S

0   50   100 mi

0   50   100 150 km

TFK TOP 5

1 **Highest point:** Granite Peak, 12,799 feet (3,904 m)

2 **Shortest river:** Roe River, 200 feet (61 m)

3 **Largest lake:** Flathead Lake, 189 sq mi (490 sq km)

4 **Largest snowflake:** 15 inches (38 cm), Fort Keogh, January 28, 1887

5 **Largest freshwater spring:** Giant Springs, with a daily flow of 156 million to 190 million gallons (590 million to 719 million L) of water

Granite Peak is one of the hardest mountains to climb in the U.S.

Montana

Nevada

Some Native American petroglyphs (rock carvings) in the Valley of Fire may be at least 1,500 years old.

NEVADA is the most arid state in the Union, getting an average of only 7 ½ inches (19 cm) of rain a year. So it's no surprise that water is Nevada's most important resource. Taking up most of Nevada is the Great Basin, a series of low-lying areas into which rivers flow, forming small lakes that dry up in the heat. Nevada's hottest, driest areas are in the south and south-central parts of the state, site of the Black Rock Desert and the Mojave Desert. The Colorado River supplies water to Nevada, as it does to other western and southwestern states. How the water is shared among the states has become a big issue.

Lake Mead is the state's largest body of water. Located in the southeast, it was formed by Hoover Dam, which backed up the Colorado River. By the time Hoover Dam was completed in 1936, it had drawn many workers to southern Nevada. Nearby Las Vegas became an important city when casinos were built there. (Nevada made gambling legal in 1931.) Now Las Vegas is a world-famous gambling and entertainment center.

THE FACT FILE

Area: 109,806 sq mi (284,397 sq km)
Population: 2,565,382
Capital: Carson City
Largest cities (with population):
Las Vegas (558,880)
Henderson (249,386)
Reno (214,853)
Entered Union (rank):
October 31, 1864 (36)
Motto: All for our country
Tree: single-leaf piñon and bristlecone pine
Flower: sagebrush
Bird: mountain bluebird
Postal code: NV

DID YOU KNOW?

● Area 51 is a top-secret military base in southern Nevada that tests experimental aircraft and weapons. Some people believe it contains an alien flying saucer that crashed in Roswell, New Mexico!

● At 1,149 feet (350 m) high, the Stratosphere Tower, in Las Vegas, is the tallest free-standing observation tower in the U.S. It's also the second tallest structure west of the Mississippi River.

● More marriages are performed in Nevada than any other state.

The brightly lit Las Vegas Strip has many hotels and casinos.

Hoover Dam is 726 feet (221 m) high. Behind it is Lake Mead, which is 110 miles (177 km) long.

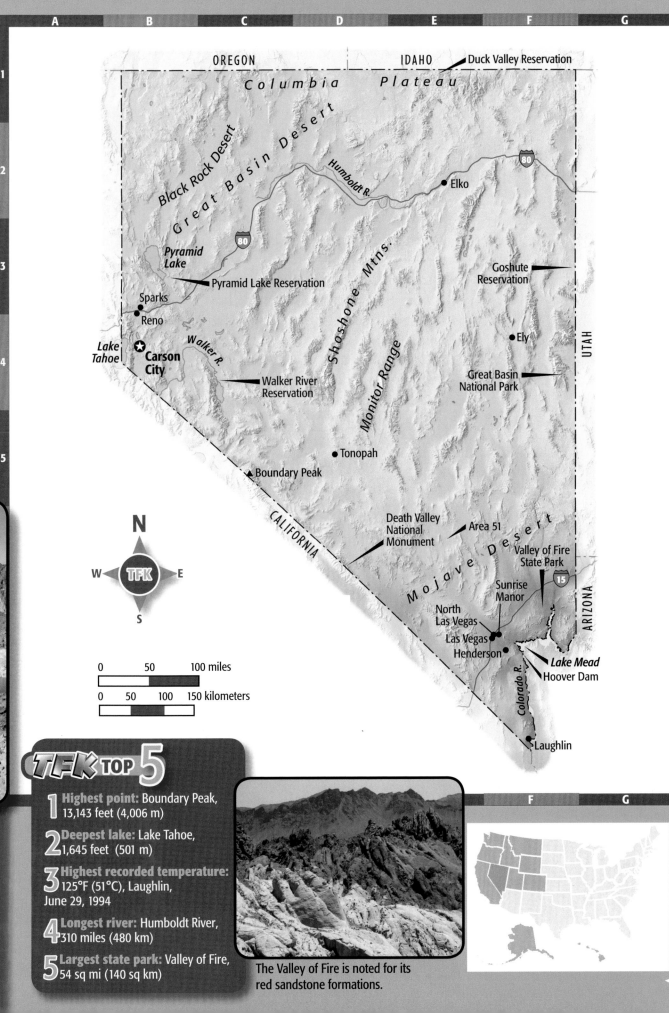

A | B | C | D | E | F | G

OREGON   IDAHO   Duck Valley Reservation

C o l u m b i a   P l a t e a u

Black Rock Desert

Great Basin Desert

Humboldt R.

80

● Elko

Pyramid Lake

Pyramid Lake Reservation

Goshute Reservation

Sparks ●

Reno ●

● Ely

Lake Tahoe

★ **Carson City**

Walker R.

Walker River Reservation

Great Basin National Park

Shoshone Mtns.

Monitor Range

UTAH

● Tonopah

▲ Boundary Peak

CALIFORNIA

N
W — TFK — E
S

Death Valley National Monument

Area 51

Mojave Desert

Valley of Fire State Park

15

ARIZONA

Sunrise Manor

North Las Vegas

Las Vegas ●

Henderson ●

➤ *Lake Mead*
Hoover Dam

Colorado R.

● Laughlin

0   50   100 miles

0   50   100   150 kilometers

TFK TOP 5

1 **Highest point:** Boundary Peak, 13,143 feet (4,006 m)

2 **Deepest lake:** Lake Tahoe, 1,645 feet (501 m)

3 **Highest recorded temperature:** 125°F (51°C), Laughlin, June 29, 1994

4 **Longest river:** Humboldt River, 310 miles (480 km)

5 **Largest state park:** Valley of Fire, 54 sq mi (140 sq km)

The Valley of Fire is noted for its red sandstone formations.

Oregon

In the 1840s, settlers heading west from Missouri took the Oregon Trail to the land of their dreams. Today, Oregon remains a great destination for those who seek its high-tech jobs, relaxed way of life and natural beauty. Oregonians appreciate what they have: they have been leaders in passing laws to protect the environment. Nearly half of Oregon is forest, and the lumber industry is important to the economy. Even so, Oregon lawmakers have put limits on logging.

Oregon's beauty comes in all forms. Along the west coast, hemmed in by the Cascade Mountains, there are long stretches of beaches and cliffs. In the northwestern part of the state is the 115 mile (185 km) Willamette Valley, formed by the Willamette River. Almost three-quarters of Oregonians live here, enjoying its mild, moist climate and rich farmland. East of the Cascades is the Columbia Plateau, a dry region formed by an ancient lava flow. Farms here grow wheat, and there are cattle ranches as well. Southeast Oregon is desert that is home to raptors—birds of prey such as hawks and eagles—but not many people.

THE FACT FILE

Area: 96,003 sq mi (248,647 sq km)
Population: 3,747,455
Capital: Salem
Largest cities (with population):
Portland (550,396)
Salem (151,913)
Eugene (149,004)
Entered Union (rank):
February 14. 1859 (33)
Motto: *Alis volat propriis*
(She flies with her own wings)
Tree: Douglas fir
Flower: Oregon grape
Bird: western meadowlark
Postal code: OR

DID YOU KNOW?

● The shoe company Nike, which is headquartered in Beaverton, is named after the Greek goddess of victory.

● During World War II, many Japanese Americans were forced to live in internment camps in Oregon. Although these people, many of whom were born in the U.S., had done nothing wrong, they weren't released until the end of the war.

● Oregon has the only state flag with a different design on each side.

Mount Hood is a dormant volcano about 50 miles (80 km) from Portland.

Multnomah Falls is the second highest year-round waterfall in the U.S.

Crater Lake, in southern Oregon, is 1,932 feet (589 m) deep.

N
W — TFK — E
S

0   50   100 mi
0   50   100   150 km

1

2

3   WASHINGTON

Columbia River

84

Umatilla Reservation

Portland

Hillsboro
Beaverton   Gresham

Multnomah Falls

▲ Mt. Hood

Pendleton

La Grande

Warm Springs Reservation

Willamette River

★ **Salem**

Willamette Valley

Corvallis

Cascade Range

Coast Range

Pacific Ocean

Eugene

5

Coos Bay

Crater Lake

Crater Lake National Park

Alvord Desert

Medford
Ashland

Klamath Falls

Old Perpetual

CALIFORNIA   NEVADA

Blue Mountains

Snake River

IDAHO

3

4

5

6

7

A   B   C   D   E   F   G

TFK TOP 5

1 **Highest point:** Mount Hood, 11,239 feet (3,425 m)

2 **Highest waterfall:** Multnomah Falls, 620 feet (189 m)

3 **Deepest lake:** Crater Lake, 1,932 feet (589 m)

4 **Highest geyser:** Old Perpetual, Lakeview, 60 feet (18 m)

5 **Tallest tree:** coastal Douglas fir, 329 feet (100 m)

ROADSIDE FUN

It's easy to see Mill Ends Park in a day. Actually, you can see all of it in the blink of an eye. Located next to Waterfront Park in Portland, this is the world's smallest park. It is 24 inches (61 cm) wide and was created by Dick Fagan in 1948 by filling in a hole in a street median with flowers. Since then, people have added a tiny swimming pool, a diving board for butterflies and a miniature Ferris wheel.

Utah

The Wasatch Mountains loom over the Great Salt Lake.

A religious group called the Church of Jesus Christ of Latter-day Saints, or Mormons, settled in **UTAH** around the middle of the 1840s. Today, Mormons make up 70 percent of the state's population. Utah is called the Beehive State because Mormons believe in working as hard as bees in a hive.

The first Mormons settled just west of the Wasatch Mountains. This area is the most populous part of Utah, because rain and runoff from the mountains keep the land green. The rest of the state is hard to live in but worth exploring. Southern Utah contains amazing rocks that wind and water have carved into dramatic shapes. Western Utah was once covered by a huge salt lake called Lake Bonneville. It dried up thousands of years ago, leaving only the Great Salt Lake and the Bonneville Salt Flats. The Salt Flats are made of packed-down salty soil where no living thing can grow. It is so smooth and vast that race-car drivers use it to set land speed records. If you stand in its midst and look at the horizon, you can see the curve of the Earth.

THE FACT FILE

Area: 82,168 sq mi (212,816 sq km)

Population: 2,645,330

Capital: Salt Lake City

Largest cities (with population): Salt Lake City (180,651) West Valley City (122,374) Provo (117,592)

Entered Union (rank): January 4, 1896 (45)

Motto: Industry

Tree: blue spruce

Flower: sego lily

Bird: California gull

Postal code: UT

DID YOU KNOW?

● The east and west tracks of the first intercontinental railway were joined at Promontory Point, Utah, on May 10, 1869. Here the Central Pacific and Union Pacific railway lines were joined after four years of construction.

● The average height of Utah's mountain peaks is the highest average of any state by 11,222 feet (3,420 m).

● Utah is the site of the biggest human-made pit in the world—the Bingham Canyon Mine. Dug by a copper company, it is about 1/2 mile (.8 km) deep and 2 1/2 miles (4 km) wide.

TFK TOP 5

1 **Highest point:** Kings Peak, 13,528 feet (4,123 m)

2 **Longest river:** Green River, about 450 miles (724 km) in Utah

3 **Lowest point:** Beaver Dam Wash, 2,178 feet (664 m)

4 **Largest natural rock span:** Rainbow Bridge, 278 feet (85 m) wide, 309 feet (94 m) high

5 **Largest lake:** Great Salt Lake, about 1,700 sq mi (4,400 sq km)

Since 1906, more than 16 million tons of copper have been removed from the Bingham Canyon Mine.

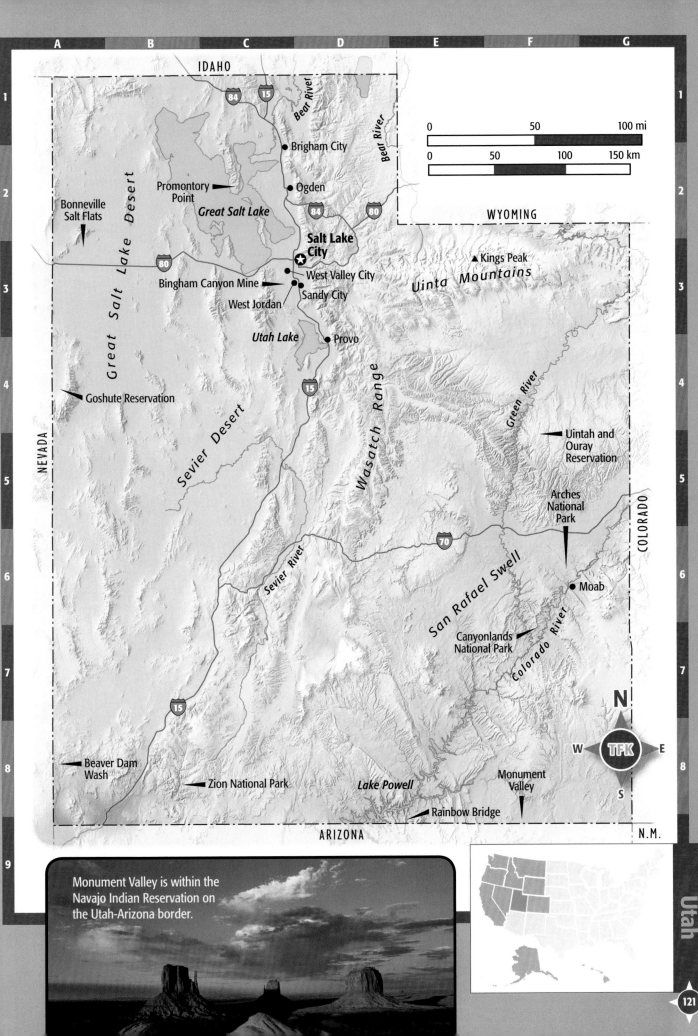

A B C D E F G

IDAHO

1

84 15

Bear River

Brigham City

Bear River

0   50   100 mi

0   50   100   150 km

2

Promontory
Point

Bonneville
Salt Flats

Great Salt Lake

Ogden

84

80

WYOMING

2

Salt Lake
City

Kings Peak

Uinta Mountains

80

West Valley City

Bingham Canyon Mine

Sandy City

West Jordan

3

Great Salt Lake Desert

NEVADA

Utah Lake

Provo

4

Goshute Reservation

15

Sevier Desert

Wasatch Range

Green River

Uintah and
Ouray
Reservation

5

Arches
National
Park

COLORADO

6

Sevier River

70

San Rafael Swell

Moab

Colorado River

Canyonlands
National Park

7

15

8

Beaver Dam
Wash

Zion National Park

Lake Powell

Rainbow Bridge

Monument
Valley

N

W TFK E

S

ARIZONA

N.M.

9

Monument Valley is within the
Navajo Indian Reservation on
the Utah-Arizona border.

Washington

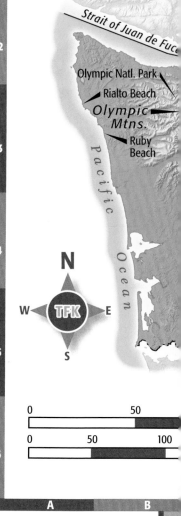

WASHINGTON is two states in one. The mountains of the Cascade Range run right down the middle of the state. West of the Cascades, the region is damp, green and lush. Because of warm ocean currents, the climate is mild. The northwest boasts the only rain forest in the U.S. The west coast is about 150 miles (241 km) long, but because of many sounds and waterways, the shoreline is much longer. About two-thirds of Washingtonians live around Puget Sound.

East of the Cascades, the state is dry and flat, even desertlike in places. But thanks to the Grand Coulee Dam, much of eastern Washington can be irrigated. This makes it possible for farmers to grow wheat and plant apple orchards. Trees are important to Washington. They cover about 30 percent of the state. Lumber is the state's biggest industry. But software companies like Microsoft have also been making Washington a center for high-tech industry.

THE FACT FILE

Area: 66,582 sq mi (172,447 sq km)
Population: 6,468,424
Capital: Olympia
Largest cities (with population):
Seattle (594,210)
Spokane (200,975)
Tacoma (196,975)
Entered Union (rank):
November 11, 1889 (42)
Motto: Al-ki (Indian word meaning "by and by")
Tree: western hemlock
Flower: coast rhododendron
Bird: willow goldfinch
Postal code: WA

DID YOU KNOW?

● Seattle's Space Needle was built for the 1962 World's Fair. At 605 feet (184 m), it was once the tallest building in the Pacific Northwest.

● The biggest building in the world by volume is the Boeing airplane-manufacturing plant in Everett. All of Disneyland could fit inside of it.

● The U.S. record for the greatest amount of snowfall in one year is 95 feet (29 m), set at Washington's Mount Baker Ski Area between July 1998 and June 1999.

Known as the Emerald City, Seattle gave birth to grunge music and Starbucks.

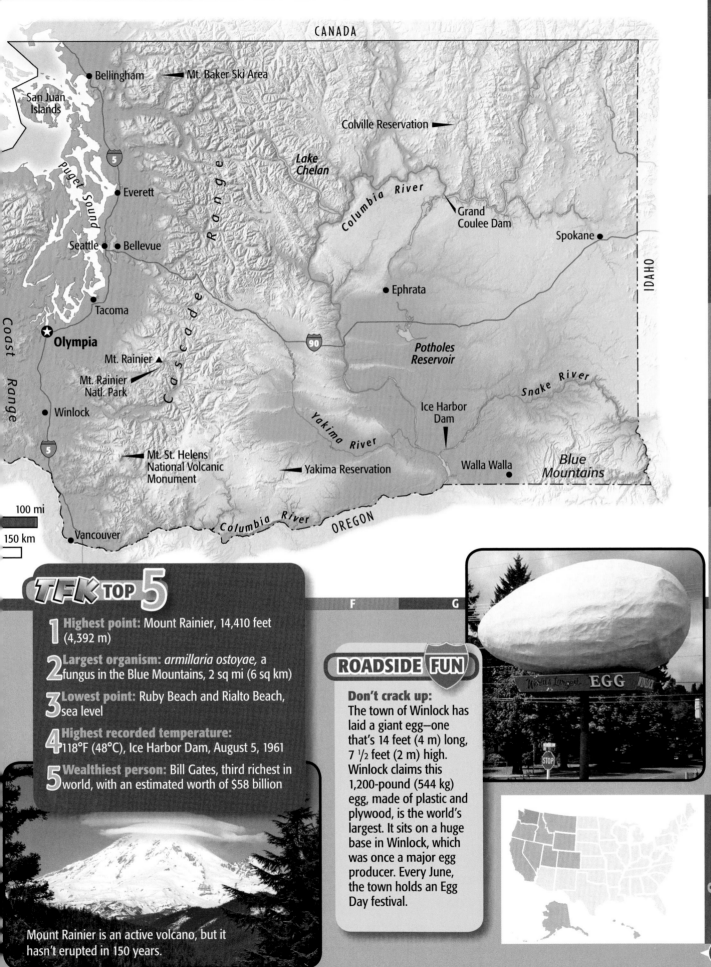

CANADA

• Bellingham → Mt. Baker Ski Area

San Juan
Islands

Colville Reservation ►

*Lake
Chelan*

Columbia River

• Everett

Grand
Coulee Dam

Seattle • • Bellevue

• Spokane

Tacoma •

• Ephrata

☆ **Olympia**

IDAHO

Mt. Rainier ▲

*Potholes
Reservoir*

Mt. Rainier
Natl. Park

Snake River

• Winlock

Ice Harbor
Dam

Mt. St. Helens
National Volcanic
Monument

→ Yakima Reservation

Yakima River

Walla Walla
•

*Blue
Mountains*

100 mi

150 km

• Vancouver

Columbia River OREGON

Puget Sound

Coast Range

Cascade Range

TFK TOP 5

1. **Highest point:** Mount Rainier, 14,410 feet
(4,392 m)

2. **Largest organism:** *armillaria ostoyae,* a
fungus in the Blue Mountains, 2 sq mi (6 sq km)

3. **Lowest point:** Ruby Beach and Rialto Beach,
sea level

4. **Highest recorded temperature:**
118°F (48°C), Ice Harbor Dam, August 5, 1961

5. **Wealthiest person:** Bill Gates, third richest in
world, with an estimated worth of $58 billion

ROADSIDE FUN

Don't crack up:
The town of Winlock has
laid a giant egg—one
that's 14 feet (4 m) long,
7 ½ feet (2 m) high.
Winlock claims this
1,200-pound (544 kg)
egg, made of plastic and
plywood, is the world's
largest. It sits on a huge
base in Winlock, which
was once a major egg
producer. Every June,
the town holds an Egg
Day festival.

World's Largest EGG

Mount Rainier is an active volcano, but it
hasn't erupted in 150 years.

Wyoming

WYOMING, like other Western states, is packed with natural beauty. Tourists come to view spectacular mountains like the Grand Tetons. Camping in Yellowstone National Park (the world's first national park) and skiing in places like Casper and Jackson Hole are popular activities. Visitors might even spend a week or two at a dude ranch, where they can learn how to be cowboys.

Wyoming has plenty of tourists but few residents. It's the ninth largest state in area but last in population. The Northern Rocky Mountains and high plateau are Wyoming's main geographical features.

THE FACT FILE

Area: 97,105 sq mi
(251,501 sq km)
Population: 522,830
Capital: Cheyenne
Largest cities (with population):
Cheyenne (55,641)
Casper (53,003)
Laramie (27,241)
Entered Union (rank):
July 10, 1890 (44)
Motto: Equal rights
Tree: cottonwood
Flower: Indian paintbrush
Bird: meadowlark
Postal code: WY

DID YOU KNOW?

● The Devils Tower (867 feet, or 264 m), in the Black Hills, is the nation's first national monument. It had a big role in the 1977 movie *Close Encounters of the Third Kind*.

● The average elevation of the state is 6,700 feet (2,044 m) above sea level, second only to Colorado.

● Wyoming is nicknamed the Equality State because, in October 1869, it became the first state to give women the right to vote and run for elected office. The first woman to win an election was Esther H. Morris, who served as justice of the peace in 1870.

Can't get to Egypt to see the pyramids? Then head out to Buford, Wyoming. Standing in the middle of nowhere is the Ames Brothers Pyramid. At 60 feet (18 m) tall and 60 feet along each side, it was built in 1882 to honor not a pharaoh but Oliver and Oakes Ames, two officials of the Union Pacific Railroad. Trains once stopped nearby, and passengers viewed the granite pyramid to kill time.

A Native American dances at the Cheyenne Frontier Days.

People who live in Wyoming are proud of its frontier history. They celebrate their past every year at a festival in Cheyenne called Cheyenne Frontier Days. Wyoming's wild beauty has inspired artists like Albert Bierstadt, Thomas Moran and Frederic Remington.

The Grand Teton Mountains rise behind a barn from the 1800s.

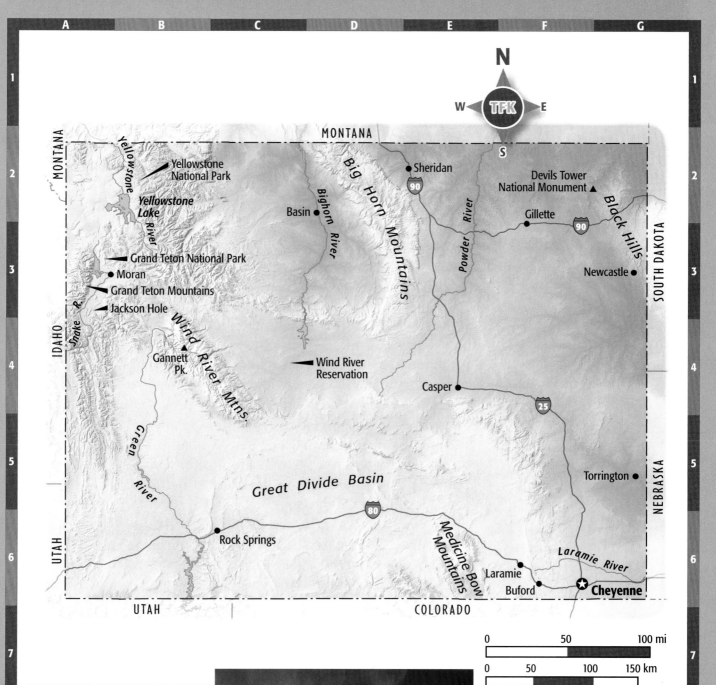

A B C D E F G

N
W—TFK—E
S

MONTANA

MONTANA

Yellowstone River

Yellowstone National Park

Yellowstone Lake

Grand Teton National Park

• Moran

Grand Teton Mountains

Jackson Hole

Snake R.

IDAHO

Wind River Mtns.

Gannett Pk. ▲

Green River

Big Horn Mountains

Bighorn River

Basin •

• Sheridan
90

Wind River Reservation

Powder River

Devils Tower National Monument ▲

Gillette •
90

Newcastle •

Black Hills

SOUTH DAKOTA

Casper •
25

Great Divide Basin
80

Rock Springs •

Medicine Bow Mountains

Torrington •

NEBRASKA

Laramie River

Laramie •
Buford •
☆ Cheyenne

UTAH

UTAH

COLORADO

0   50   100 mi
0   50   100   150 km

F G

TFK TOP 5

1 Highest point: Gannett Peak, 13,804 feet (4,210 m)

2 Highest recorded temperature: 114°F (46°C), Basin, July 12, 1900

3 Lowest recorded temperature: -63°F (-53°C), Moran, February 9, 1933

4 Highest lake: Yellowstone Lake, 7,731 feet (2,358 m) above sea level

5 Most famous outlaw: Butch Cassidy (1866-1908), Wyoming bandit who, with the Wild Bunch gang, robbed banks and stagecoaches

In Yellowstone National Park, the geyser Old Faithful shoots water about 145 feet (44 m) high.

Wyoming

125

Washington, D.C.

The **DISTRICT OF COLUMBIA** is the capital of the United States. In 1790, Congress declared that the nation's capital should be created on land between Maryland and Virginia on the Potomac River. In 1800, the capital was moved from Philadelphia to the city of Washington, which sat within the larger District of Columbia (D.C.). In 1871, Washington and D.C. were combined as one city, Washington, D.C. Today, Washington is a city of long avenues and grand monuments made of marble. It is home to many national organizations and foreign embassies. Washington's main businesses are the Federal government and tourism. Visitors can see the three branches of government at work at the White House, the Capitol building and the Supreme Court building. The Smithsonian Institution draws millions of people to its 14 museums (which include the National Zoo). Other attractions include the Washington Monument, the Jefferson Memorial, the Lincoln Memorial and the Vietnam Veterans Memorial. The Declaration of Independence, the Constitution and the Bill of Rights are on display at the National Archives.

THE FACT FILE

Area: 68 sq mi (177 sq km)
Population: 588,292
Motto: *Justitia omnibus* (Justice to all)
Tree: scarlet oak
Flower: American beauty rose
Bird: wood thrush
Established: June 11, 1800

DID YOU KNOW?

● French architect Pierre Charles L'Enfant worked on the original plan for the city of Washington in 1791, but he was fired before he could finish the job. Freeborn African American astronomer, mathematician and surveyor Benjamin Banneker helped complete the design of the city.

● George Washington is the only President never to have lived in the White House. In 1800, John Adams was the first President to move into what was then called the President's House when the building was nearly completed.

● Residents of Washington, D.C., didn't have the right to vote in presidential elections until 1961, when the 23rd Amendment to the Constitution was ratified.

From the steps of the U.S. Capitol (near right), visitors can see the Lincoln Memorial (below) and the Washington Monument (far right).

TFK TOP 5

1 Highest structure: Washington Monument, 555 feet (169 m)

2 Biggest building: Ronald Reagan Building and International Trade Center, 3.1 million sq ft (287,999 sq m)

3 Oldest House: The Old Stone House, built in 1765 in Georgetown

4 Highest point: Tenleytown, 420 feet (128 m)

5 Highest recorded temperature: 106°F (41°C), July 1930

The Vietnam Veterans Memorial honors fallen soldiers.

U.S. Territories

A **TERRITORY** is a region that belongs to the U.S but is not one of the 50 states. Territories are allowed to govern themselves in a limited way, but the U.S. government is the ultimate authority. Puerto Rico, in the Caribbean Sea, is the largest territory (see below). The U.S. Virgin Islands, which are made of three main islands (St. Croix, St. Thomas and St. John) and about 50 tiny islands, were bought from Denmark in 1917. In the Pacific region, Guam, the largest and southernmost island in the Mariana Island chain, became a U.S. territory in 1898. The Northern Mariana Islands have been part of the U.S. since 1986, and include the inhabited islands of Rota, Saipan and Tinian. American Samoa is a group of five volcanic islands and two coral atolls, and includes three eastern Samoan islands and three islands of the Manu'a group, as well as Swains Island. The territory became part of the U.S. in 1900, except for Swains Island, which was acquired in 1925.

In addition, the U.S. owns seven very small territories—made up of tiny islands, reefs and atolls—none more than a few miles long and mostly uninhabited: Midway Islands; Wake Island (actually an atoll made up of the Wilkes, Peale and Wake islets); Johnston Atoll (made up of Johnston, Sand, Hikina and Akau islands); Baker, Howland and Jarvis islands; Kingman Reef; Navassa Island; and Palmyra Atoll.

Commonwealth of Puerto Rico

Puerto Rico has been a U.S. possession since 1898, when the U.S. took it over from Spain. Puerto Rico consists of the island of Puerto Rico and the nearby small islands of Vieques, Culebra and Mona. Although residents of Puerto Rico are U.S. citizens, they can't vote in Presidential elections.

Puerto Rico

THE FACT FILE

Area: 3,459 sq mi (8,959 sq km)
Population: 3,942,375
Capital: San Juan
Largest cities (with population):
San Juan (434,374)
Bayamón (241,142)
Carolina (187,468)
Motto: *Joannes est nomen eius* (John is his name)
Tree: ceiba (silk-cotton)
Flower: flor de Maga (Puerto Rican hibiscus)
Bird: reinita (stripe-headed tanager)
Languages: Spanish and English

DID YOU KNOW?

● 4,120,205 Puerto Ricans now live in the 50 U.S. states. For the first time, more Puerto Ricans live in the U.S. states than in Puerto Rico.

Luquillo Beach is the most popular beach in Puerto Rico.

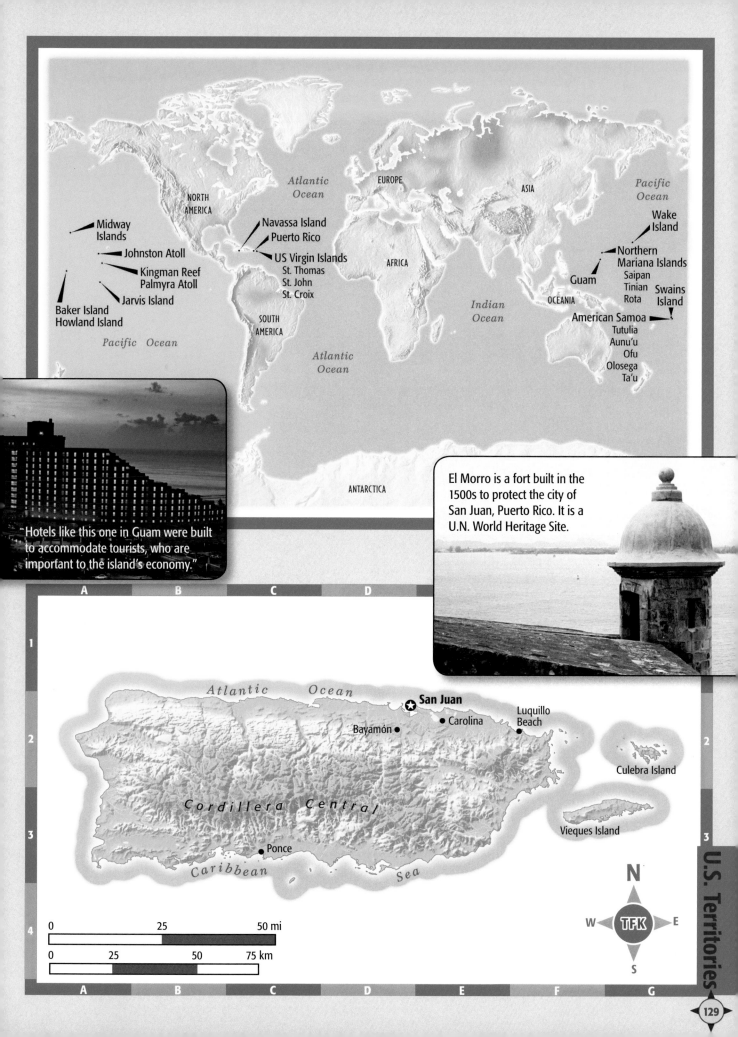

Midway
Islands

Johnston Atoll

Kingman Reef
Palmyra Atoll

Jarvis Island

Baker Island
Howland Island

Pacific Ocean

NORTH
AMERICA

*Atlantic
Ocean*

Navassa Island
Puerto Rico

US Virgin Islands
St. Thomas
St. John
St. Croix

SOUTH
AMERICA

*Atlantic
Ocean*

EUROPE

AFRICA

ASIA

*Indian
Ocean*

OCEANIA

*Pacific
Ocean*

Wake
Island

Northern
Mariana Islands
Saipan
Tinian
Rota

Guam

Swains
Island

American Samoa
Tutulia
Aunu'u
Ofu
Olosega
Ta'u

ANTARCTICA

Hotels like this one in Guam were built
to accommodate tourists, who are
important to the island's economy.

El Morro is a fort built in the
1500s to protect the city of
San Juan, Puerto Rico. It is a
U.N. World Heritage Site.

Atlantic   Ocean

⭐ **San Juan**

Bayamón ●

● Carolina

Luquillo
Beach ●

Culebra Island

Cordillera   Central

Vieques Island

● Ponce

Caribbean   Sea

0	25	50 mi

0	25	50	75 km

N
W ◆TFK◆ E
S

U.S. Facts

The bald eagle is the national bird.

THE FACT FILE

Area (including land, water and territories): 3,722,228 sq mi (9,640,526 sq km)
Population: 301,621,157 [2007 estimate]
Largest state: Alaska, 656,424 sq mi (1,700,135 sq km)
Smallest state: Rhode Island, 1,045 sq mi (2,706 sq km)
Most populous state: California, 36,553,215
Least populous state: Wyoming, 522,830
Most populous city: New York City (8,274,527)
National bird: bald eagle
National flower: rose
National anthem: "Star-Spangled Banner"
National march: "Stars and Stripes Forever" (composed by John Philip Sousa)
National motto: In God we trust
National tree: oak

PEOPLE

Top 5 Most Populous Cities
1. New York City, New York: 8,274,527
2. Los Angeles, California: 3,834,340
3. Chicago, Illinois: 2,836,658
4. Houston, Texas: 2,208,180
5. Phoenix, Arizona: 1,552,259

Ethnic/Racial Breakdown in U.S. (Self-reported)
- White: 79.9 percent of population
- Black or African American: 12.8 percent of population
- American Indian and Alaska native: 0.97 percent of population
- Asian: 4.4 percent of population
- Native Hawaiian and other Pacific Islanders: 0.17 percent of population
- Hispanic or Latino: 15 percent of population
(Adds up to more than 100 percent because Hispanic/Latino self-identify with other racial categories.)

Top 5 Reported Ancestries
1. German: 15 percent of population
2. Irish: 11 percent
3. African American: 9 percent
4. American: 7 percent
5. Mexican: 7 percent
Source: Census 2000

PEOPLE

Top 5 Birthplaces of Foreign-Born Americans
1. Mexico
2. China
3. Philippines
4. India
5. Cuba
Source: Census 2000

Top 5 States with the Highest American-Indian Population
1. Oklahoma: 285,764
2. California: 423,238
3. Arizona: 297,422
4. New Mexico: 186,256
5. Washington: 105,515
Source: Census, 2007 estimates

Top 5 Largest American-Indian Tribes
1. Cherokee
2. Navajo
3. Latin American Indian
4. Choctaw
5. Sioux

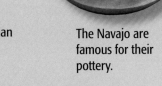

The Navajo are famous for their pottery.

Top 5 States Most Visited by Tourists
1. California
2. Florida
3. Texas
4. Pennsylvania
5. New York

PLACES

Land owned by U.S. Government, which includes National Parks, Forests and Wildlife Refuges: 1,015,625 sq mi (2,630,456 sq km), about 30 percent of U.S. land area
Points farthest apart (50 states): Log Point, Elliot Key, Florida, and Kure Island, Hawaii: 5,859 mi (9,429 km)
Geographic center (50 states): Butte County, South Dakota
Geographic center (Lower 48 states): Smith County, Kansas

Mount McKinley (Denali)

Length of U.S. Boundaries
- Between Alaska and Canada: 1,538 miles (2,475 km)
- Between Lower 48 states and Canada (including the Great Lakes): 3,987 miles (6,416 km)
- Between U.S. and Mexico: 1,933 miles (3,111 km)

State with highest average elevation: Colorado, 6,800 feet (2,072 m)

State with lowest average elevation: Delaware, 60 feet (18 m)

Largest national park: Wrangell–St. Elias, Alaska, 13,004 sq mi (33,680 sq km)

Largest national park in Lower 48: Death Valley, California, 5,219 sq mi (13,517 sq km)

Top 5 Longest Rivers
1. Mississippi River: 2,348 miles (3,779 km), from Lake Itasca in Minnesota to mouth of Southwest Pass in Louisiana
2. Missouri River: 2,315 miles (3,726 km), from meeting place of Jefferson, Gallatin and Madison rivers in Montana to Mississippi River, near St. Louis
3. Rio Grande: 1,900 miles (3,060 km), from San Juan County in Colorado to Gulf of Mexico
4. Arkansas River: 1,459 miles (2,348 km), from Lake County in Colorado to Mississippi River in Arkansas
5. Colorado River: 1,450 miles (2,333 km), from Rocky Mountain National Park in Colorado to Gulf of California in Mexico

Top 5 Largest Lakes by Area
1. Lake Superior: 31,820 sq mi (82,414 sq km)
2. Lake Huron: 23,010 sq mi (59,596 sq km)
3. Lake Michigan: 22,400 sq mi (58,016 sq km)
4. Lake Erie: 9,930 sq mi (25,719 sq km)
5. Lake Ontario: 7,520 (19,477 sq km)

Top 5 Tallest Peaks
1. Mount McKinley (Denali), Alaska: 20,320 feet (6,194 m)
2. Mount St. Elias, Alaska: 18,008 feet (5,488 m)
3. Mount Foraker, Alaska: 17,400 feet (5,303 m)
4. Mount Bona, Alaska: 16,500 feet (5,029 m)
5. Mount Blackburn, Alaska: 16,390 feet (4,995 m)

Top 5 Largest Deserts
1. Great Basin: 190,000 sq mi (492,097 sq km)–Nevada, Oregon, Utah
2. Chihuahuan Desert: 175,000 sq mi (453,247 sq km)–Mexico, New Mexico, Texas, Arizona
3. Colorado Plateau: 130,000 sq mi (336, 698 sq km)–Arizona, Colorado, New Mexico, Utah, Wyoming
4. Sonoran Desert: 120,000 sq mi (310,798 sq km)–Arizona, California, Mexico
5. Mojave Desert: 54,000 sq mi (139,859 sq km)–Arizona, Colorado, Nevada, Utah, California

Top 5 Highest Waterfalls
1. Yosemite, Yosemite National Park, California: 2,425 feet (739 m)
2. Sentinel, Yosemite National Park, California: 2,000 feet (610 m)
3. Kahiwa, Molokai, Hawaii: 1,750 feet (533 m)
4. Ribbon, Yosemite National Park, California: 1,612 feet (491 m)
5. Kaliuwaa (Sacred), Oahu, Hawaii: 1,520 feet (463 m)

INTERNET FACTS

To find more information about subjects covered in this atlas as well as other subjects related to the nation, check out these Web sites:

States
Most official state Web sites can be accessed by one of two ways: www.state.[the state's postal abbreviation].us. The other way is by www.[name of state].gov

Below, for example, are two Web sites that will take you to Alabama's official state Web site.

www.state.al.us
www.alabama.gov

For links to state governments, Washington, D.C., and U.S. territories, go to: www.usa.gov

For the Time For Kids Great State Race trivia game, go to: www.timeforkids.com/tfk/kids/games/story/0,28521,355884,00.html

CIA World Factbook, for information on the U.S.: https://www.cia.gov/library/publications/the-world-factbook/geos/us.html

Washington, D.C.
http://kids.dc.gov
White House: www.whitehouse.gov
Smithsonian Institution: www.si.edu
National Archives: www.archives.gov

Population
Census 2000: www.census.gov/main/www/cen2000.html
Census 2010: www.census.gov/2010census/
States: http://quickfacts.census.gov/qfd/
Cities: www.city-data.com

Maps
Google maps: http://earth.google.com/
Google city street views: http://maps.google.com/help/maps/streetview/
U.S. map: http://nationalmap.gov/
Night map of U.S.: http://apod.nasa.gov/apod/ap970830.html
Topographic maps: http://topomaps.usgs.gov/

Glossary

aquifer an underground layer of rock, sand or gravel that holds water

archipelago a group of scattered islands often found in isolated parts of the ocean

arid dry; usually describes a climate that can't support farming

atoll a coral island or group of coral islands often made up of a reef surrounding a lagoon

BADLANDS

badlands a region of hills with little or no vegetation and that has been eroded into unusual shapes

barrier reef a long sandy island that protects a near-by coast from the ocean

basin an area, sometimes very large, where the land dips down

bay a section of an ocean or lake that fills an indentation in the coastline

bayou a marshy, slow-moving river, stream or creek

bog an area of soft, wet ground

BUTTE

butte an isolated hill or mountain with steep sides; smaller than a mesa

canal a human-made waterway

canyon a deep valley with steep sides, often formed by a river

contiguous United States the 48 states on the North American landmass that all border each other; also known as the Lower 48; excludes Alaska and Hawaii

continental United States the 49 states on the North American landmass; all the U.S. states except for Hawaii

CRATER

crater a bowl-shaped depression in the land

delta an area of land formed where a river flows into a larger body of water; made of soil, sand and small rocks carried there by the flowing river

Delta a large area of northwestern Mississippi, between the Mississippi and Yazoo rivers, noted for its rich soil

desert an area of land that receives little rain, snow or other precipitation

drift clay, sand or gravel left behind by a glacier

estuary a body of water where saltwater from the ocean mixes with freshwater from a river

fjord a narrow inlet of a sea bordered by steep cliffs

glacier a large, slow-moving sheet of ice

gorge a narrow canyon with steep walls

grassland land where there is enough rain to support grass but not a lot of trees

gulf a large bay

GLACIER

HOT SPRING

hot spring a stream of hot water that flows naturally from out of the ground

loess rich soil that has been carried to an area by the wind

marsh soft, wet land

mesa an isolated, elevated section of land that is flat-topped; it's wider than a butte but smaller than a plateau

peninsula land surrounded on three sides by water

piedmont a gently hilly region that slowly rises to the mountains

plains large, flat landscape with few trees

plateau a large, flat area that is higher than the surrounding land

prairie flat or rolling land that is covered by grass

rangeland land on which livestock graze

reef a ridge of sand or a chain of coral at or near the water's surface

RESERVOIR

reservoir a human-made lake where water is collected and stored for use, such as for drinking water

ridge a range of hills or mountains

rural like the country; open and without many people

sound a long area of water that separates an island from the mainland

strait a narrow strip of water connecting two larger bodies of water

swamp low ground that is filled with, and often covered by, water

till a combination of gravel, sand, clay and boulders left behind by glaciers

tributary a stream or river that flows into a larger stream or river

urban of, or relating to, a city

valley a length of lowland often with a stream or river flowing through it

WETLAND

wetland an area, including bogs, swamps and marshes, covered by water

wilderness natural land undisturbed by people

State Your Case

Y ou're invited to take part in a U.S. scavenger hunt. The goal is to answer 25 questions about the states, and all the information you need is in this book. Write each answer in the boxes provided. When you're finished, the letters in the shaded boxes will spell out the answer to this riddle: **WHAT DID TENNESSEE?** The answer is on page 144.

Pennsylvania

1. Oaks Amusement Park is located in what Oregon city?

2. The Palisades in New Jersey overlooks what river?

3. What New England state is the third smallest in area of all U.S. states?

4. What does the motto of Montana mean in English?

5. What Midwestern state almost always leads the U.S. in wheat production?

6. What city in Oregon has a population of 151,913?

7. What is the tallest mountain in the Pacific Ocean?

8. What large reservoir is west of the Mississippi Petrified Forest?

9. In what North Carolina town is the largest privately owned house in the U.S.?

10. The population of which Southwest state has the highest percentage of Hispanics in the U.S.?

11. Over which New England state does the sun first rise each morning?

Vermont

12. What sea is on the west coast of Alaska?

13. In which Midwest state does the Mississippi River begin?

[ ][ ][ ][ ][ ][ ][ ][ ][ ]

14. What is the highest point in the U.S.?

[ ][ ][ ][ ][ ][ ]   [ ][ ][ ][ ][ ][ ][ ][ ]

15. Interstate Highway 75 crosses the northern border of Kentucky into which state?

[ ][ ][ ][ ]

16. Of the two states that share Hoover Dam, which is located farther west?

[ ][ ][ ][ ][ ][ ]

17. What southern state borders on eight other states?

[ ][ ][ ][ ][ ][ ][ ][ ][ ]

18. Harrisburg is the capital of what Northeast state?

[ ][ ][ ][ ][ ][ ][ ][ ][ ][ ][ ][ ]

19. What is the only New England state without a seacoast?

[ ][ ][ ][ ][ ][ ][ ]

20. What is the largest lake in Florida?

[ ][ ][ ][ ][ ]   [ ][ ][ ][ ][ ][ ][ ][ ][ ][ ]

21. What river forms the border between Texas and Mexico?

[ ][ ][ ][ ]   [ ][ ][ ][ ][ ][ ]

22. What is the postal code of Nebraska?

[ ][ ]

23. What is the largest lake in Utah?

[ ][ ][ ][ ][ ][ ]   [ ][ ][ ][ ][ ]   [ ][ ][ ][ ][ ]

24. Which southwestern state was the last Lower 48 state to have entered the Union?

[ ][ ][ ][ ][ ][ ][ ][ ]

25. What western state is called the Evergreen State?

[ ][ ][ ][ ][ ][ ][ ][ ][ ][ ]

Arizona

Nevada

Utah

Capital Idea

Nineteen state capitals are hidden in this word-search grid. They can be found going up, down, forward and backward. Listed below are the names of all the capitals in the grid. When you've solved the puzzle, look at the leftover letters. What is the state whose capital is spelled out? The answer is on page 144.

```
O  J  J  S  E  N  I  O  M  S  E  D  Y
K  U  E  U  L  U  L  O  N  O  H  T  T
L  N  O  T  S  E  L  R  A  H  C  R  I
A  E  G  U  O  R  N  O  T  A  B  O  C
H  A  R  R  I  S  B  U  R  G  L  F  E
O  U  F  E  S  I  O  B  F  S  A  K  K
M  E  R  S  S  I  L  O  P  A  N  N  A
A  U  S  T  I  N  O  S  N  L  S  A  L
C  N  O  T  N  E  R  T  C  E  I  R  T
I  S  U  B  M  U  L  O  C  M  N  F  L
T  H  E  L  E  N  A  N  I  T  G  Y  A
Y  T  A  L  L  A  H  A  S  S  E  E  S
```

Juneau	Tallahassee	Honolulu	Boise
Des Moines	Frankfort	Baton Rouge	Annapolis
Boston	Lansing	Helena	Trenton
Columbus	Oklahoma City	Salem	Harrisburg
Austin	Salt Lake City	Charleston	

United Mistakes

Can you identify these five states just by their shapes? To make things more difficult, we've turned some of the states upside down and sideways. We've also made them different sizes—some states are drawn bigger than they should be, others are drawn smaller. If you name all five correctly, you might have a career in mapmaking! The answers are on page 144.

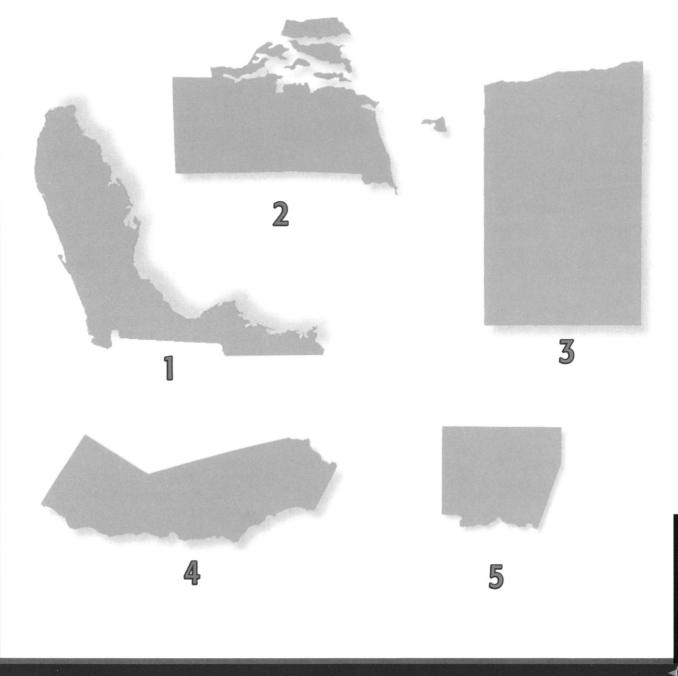

1

2

3

4

5

Index

Credits

Key: (S) = Shutterstock
All photos clockwise from top left
All state flags: Martine Oger (S)
Cover: Mahesh Patil (S); Dmitry Ruthlenko (S); Pontus Edenberg (S); Gary Paul Lewis (S); urosr (S); ErickN (S); Jim Nelson (S); globe: digitalife (S)
Back cover: Michael Shake (S); Douglas Knight (S); dtcdthingy, public domain; Mario Savoia (S); Mikhail A. Shifrin (S)
Title page: Ivan Cholatov (S); Matthew Luzitano (S); Christian Musat (S); Arthur Snyder-Bell (S); MM5 (S)
2-3: surfer: Mana Photo (S); Stephen Finn (S); Mark William Penny (S); gary718 (S); Peter Digre (S)
4-5: compass: Galusho Sergey (S)
6-7: Ken Durden (S); Donald R. Swartz (S); Karen Gentry (S)
8-9: John A. Anderson (S); Robert Kylio (S); John Kroetch (S); Galeb Foster (S); Kenneth V. Pilon (S)
10-11: Kenneth V. Pilon (S)
12-13: George Pappas (S); Richard Sargeant (S); Greg McCracken (S); William Casey (S); Joy Fera (S)
14-15: NASA
16-17: Sparkling Moments Photography (S); Dana Ward (S); C. Kurt Holter (S); stocklight (S)
18-19: Arthur Connors (S); Brett Rabideau (S); Jeffrey M. Frank (S)
20-21: Andrew Williams (S); Tim Kiser; A. L. Spangler (S)
22-23: Doug Lemke (S); Matthew Luzitano (S); Stephen G. Page (S)
24-25: APaterson (S); An Van de Wal (S); Henry E. Stamm IV (S)
26-27: Christopher Penler (S); David Schnerch (S)
28-29: Thomas & Amelia Takacs (S); Patricia Hofmeester (S); Robert Manley (S); Michael Shake (S)
30-31: Izzat Bakhadyrov (S); gary718 (S); dtcdthingy, public domain; gary718 (S)
32-33: Jonathan Esper (S); Lori Froeb (S); Michael Shake (S); gary718 (S)
34-35: Jospeh Gareri (S); Natalia Bratslavsky (S); Laurie Barr (S)
36-37: Katherine Welles (S); Travel Bug (S); Mona Makela (S)
38-39: Chee-Onn Leong (S); Marcio Jose Bastos Silva (S)
40-41: Joe Gough (S); Wendy Kaveney Photography (S); Lawrence Roberg (S); Rena Schild (S)
42-43: Danny E. Hooks (S); Wikipedia, public domain; LouLouPhotos (S); LouLouPhotos (S)
44-45: Travel Bug (S); Lori Martin (S); Jonathan Brizendine (S)
46-47: newphotoservice (S); coralcastle.com; L. S. Luecke (S); Allen Furmanski (S)
48-49: Mark William Penny (S); Nickd, public domain; jackweichen_gatech (S); Alexphoto (S)

50-51: Cheryl Ann Quigley (S); Alexey Stiop (S); Alexey Stiop (S)
52-53: Lori Monahan Borden (S); Kathryn Bell (S); Kevin D. Oliver (S)
54-55: Andrea Skjold (S); Stephan de Prouw (S); John C. Panella Jr (S); Rick Lord (S)
56-57: Audrey Snyder-Bell (S); John Marshall; Ammon Andrew Cogdill (S); Patrick Johnson (S)
58-59: Samot (S); Travel Bug (S); Beth Whitcomb (S); Beth Whitcomb (S)
60-61: David S. Baker (S); Jennifer King (S); Mary Terriberry (S)
62-63: Carolyn M. Carpenter (S); U.S. Department of Defense; Graham S. Klotz (S)
64-65: Lora Clark (S); Henryk Sadura (S); Jerry Whaley (S); Amanda Haddox (S)
66-67: Jim Parkin (S); Winthrop Brookhouse (S); Weldon Schloneger (S)
68-69: Mario Savoia (S); Ian D. Walker (S); Henryk Sadura (S)
70-71: Thomas Barrat (S); amygdala imagery (S); ciapix (S)
72-73: Madeleine Openshaw (S); Craig Markley, Iowa Dept. of Transportation; Steve Adamson (S)
74-75: Ivan Cholakov (S); Bart Everett (S); Rusty Dodson (S)
76-77: mypokcik (S); Thomas Barrat (S); Vladimir Mucibabic (S); Robert Gubbins (S)
78-79: zaiel photography (S); Vladimir Daragan (S); Near and Far Photography (S)
80-81: Steve Byland (S); Jothi Pallikkathayit (S); Sharon Day (S); Mike Liu (S)
82-83: Henryk Sadura (S); World's Largest Things, Inc.; IntraClique, LLC (S)
84-85: Rusty Dodson (S); MatthewUND; Trutta (S)
86-87: Denise Kappa (S); aceshot1 (S); Robert J. Daveant (S)
88-89: dakotaboy (S); Oralleff (S); Peter Digre (S)
90-91: Jill Battaglia (S); Henryk Sadura (S); John S. Sfondilas (S)
92-93: Stephen Finn (S); PSHAW-Photo (S); Mikhail A. Shifrin (S)
94-95: Jim Parkin (S); Joao Virissimo (S); Kenneth V. Pilon (S)
96-97: Douglas Knight (S); Cousin_Avi (S); MM5 (S)
98-99: Ron Hilton (S); White Pelican; Lori Martin (S); Patrick W. Mitchell (S)
100-101: Mastering_Microstock (S); Donna Beeler (S); Roni Lias (S); Toilet Seat Art Museum; Patricia Marroquin (S)
102-103: Valery Pottorak (S); Katrina Brown (S); Andy Z (S)
104-105: Terence Mendoza (S); MaxFX (S); Marko Hevver (S)
106-107: Christian Musat (S); Zack Frank (S); Mike Norton (S); City of Lathrop, CA
108-109: Natasha Currlin Japp (S); George Burba (S); Evan Meyer (S)
110-111: Mana Photo (S); Dan Lee (S); Jeanne Hatch (S); Jennie Endriss (S); TechWizard (S)
112-113: Jennifer Leigh Selig (S); LSgrd42 (S); eyespeak (S); Pierdelune (S)
114-115: Catherine Lall (S); Clara (S); Donny Hahn (S)

116-117: slowfish (S); Stephen Coburn (S); slowfish (S); Helen & Vlad Filatov (S)
118-119: Jeff Banke (S); Wikipedia, public domain; zschnepf (S); Winthrop Brookhouse (S)
120-121: Tony Strong (S); Dallas Events, Inc. (S); Rafa Irusta (S)
122-123: Stephen Strathdee (S); Chuck Woodbury; Paula Cobleigh (S); Adrian Baras (S)
124-125: Jack Boucher; kavram (S); David Kocherhaus (S); Lincoln Rogers (S)
126-127: U.S. Government; MBWTE Photos (S); Jonathan Larsen (S); Yehuda Boltshauser (S)
128-129: Keith Tarrier (S); Cristi Bastian (S); ciapix (S)
130-131: Eric Gevaert (S); Diane N. Ennis (S); TTphoto (S)
132-133: MaxFX (S); Mike Norton (S); kavram (S); Katrina Brown (S); Joao Virissimo (S); Audrey Levedeb (S); Steven Coburn (S)
134-135: Jim Parkin (S); Helen & Vlad Filatov (S); Tony Strong (S); Chee-Onn Leong (S); Natalia Bratslavsky (S)

Answers

State Your Case: 1. Portland; 2. Hudson River; 3. Connecticut; 4. gold and silver; 5. Kansas; 6. Salem; 7. Mauna Kea; 8. Ross Barnett Reservoir; 9. Asheville; 10. New Mexico; 11. Maine; 12. Bering Sea; 13. Minnesota; 14. Mount McKinley; 15. Ohio; 16. Nevada; 17. Tennessee; 18. Pennsylvania; 19. Vermont; 20. Lake Okeechobee; 21. Rio Grande; 22. NE, 23; Great Salt Lake; 24. Arizona; 25. Washington. The answer to the riddle is: The same things that Arkansas.

Capital Idea: Missouri (its capital is Jefferson City)

O	J	S	E	N	I	O	M	S	E	D	Y	
K	U	E	U	L	U	L	O	N	O	H	T	I
L	N	O	T	S	E	L	R	A	H	C	R	I
A	E	G	U	O	R	N	O	T	A	G	I	C
H	A	R	R	I	S	B	U	R	G	L	F	E
O	U	F	E	S	I	O	B	F	S	A	K	K
M	E	R	S	I	L	O	P	A	N	N	A	A
A	U	S	T	I	N	O	S	N	L	S	A	L
C	N	O	T	N	E	R	T	C	E	I	R	T
I	S	U	B	M	U	L	O	C	M	N	F	L
T	H	E	L	E	N	A	N	I	T	G	Y	A
Y	T	A	L	L	A	H	A	S	S	E	E	S

United Mistakes:
1. Florida; 2. Rhode Island; 3. North Dakota; 4. California; 5. Arizona